THE COMPLETE GUIDE TO BUYING

Repossessed Property Bargains

Catherine Dawson

The Complete Guide to Buying Repossessed Property Bargains
by Catherine Dawson

© 2008 Lawpack Publishing

Lawpack Publishing Limited
76–89 Alscot Road
London SE1 3AW

www.lawpack.co.uk

ISBN: 978-1-905261-79-6

Exclusion of Liability and Disclaimer

Contents

About the author

Catherine Dawson is a trained and experienced researcher with an MA in Social Research. Her speciality is housing issues and she is the author of several books on property, including *Investing in Property for your Children*, also published by Lawpack. Since 1996 she has been a shareholder of a growing and successful family property development company for which she conducts the research and development. This includes collecting information about the repossession procedure and developing successful strategies to obtain bargain properties.

Acknowledgements

I would like to thank A P Malam Property Lawyers (www.apmalam.co.uk) for their kind help in the research for Chapter 10, and for providing much useful information and friendly advice about the conveyancing process and repossessed property.

Introduction

> '*My partner and I really wanted to find out about repossessed properties, but we just didn't know where to start, and our local estate agent was no help at all. He said that there was nothing available, took our names and addresses and we never heard from him again. Where do you go for the information? We're sure that there must be bargains about but we just don't know how you find out about them.*'
>
> **Kath and Steve, Bristol.**

Many house-hunters, like Kath and Steve, believe there are repossessed properties on the market that provide a bargain, especially for people who may be struggling to step onto the property ladder or who are finding it difficult to keep up with property price rises in their area. But many point out that it is almost impossible to find out what is available, on both a national and local level. There is no central database of repossessed properties for sale in the UK and estate agents and lenders seem reluctant or unwilling to advertise property as 'repossessed'.

Kath and Steve are right in believing that there are repossessed bargains available. In some cases it is possible to buy a property at ten to 15 per cent below market value. This is because the lender that has repossessed the property needs to make a quick sale to recover the money it has loaned, and it may be willing to accept a lower offer on the property. Also, some properties that have been repossessed are in a poor state of repair and are, therefore, offered more cheaply than other homes of similar type that are presented in a better condition. But, to obtain such a bargain, you may face stiff competition from property developers and investors, who may adopt rather questionable practices when obtaining bargain properties, such as paying finder's fees to estate agents. So you need to know where to look for properties and understand the best ways to achieve success when you find a property you like.

This book will help you to do this by providing a practical, user-friendly guide to buying a repossessed property for residential use. It covers everything you need to know about buying a property, from knowing where to look, to understanding how to negotiate with estate agents and lenders, or buying a property at auction. It explains the repossession process so that you can understand how to make a bid for a property and the process through which a property could be advertised, once you have made a bid. It also discusses the problems you may face if you choose to buy a repossessed property and the action you can take to reduce or avoid these problems.

Once you have read this book you will be able to:

- know how to find out about repossessed properties;

- understand the bidding procedure;

- choose the right property and avoid properties with too many problems;

- know how much a property is worth and how to make an appropriate offer;

- know how to beat the competition;

- overcome or avoid problems associated with moving into and living in a repossessed property.

Some housing experts fear that the number of repossessions in the UK will increase considerably as the 'credit crunch' begins to bite. While this is extremely unfortunate for people who have to move out of their homes, it does provide an opportunity for others to obtain a property at below market value, when they may be unable to do so otherwise. There are bargains available and, with increased knowledge and understanding, you will be able to find out about these bargains and obtain a property suitable for you and your family.

I am a shareholder in a family-run property business, for which I conduct all the research and development. Our business is always on the lookout for bargain properties, which includes those that have been repossessed. Over the years we have increased our understanding about the possession procedure and have developed successful strategies that help us to obtain properties at a bargain price. In this book I hope to pass this information on to you. I hope you enjoy reading this book and find it useful and interesting. Good luck with your property hunting.

Catherine Dawson
September 2008

CHAPTER 1:

REPOSSESSED PROPERTY: FACTS AND FIGURES

 *'Well, I've heard that there are bargains to be had, you know, properties that have been repossessed. But is it really true? Are there loads about, or is it just a myth? And what are they? Who's selling them? I certainly want to know more.'*

Michelle, first-time buyer, Weymouth.

There are many myths and rumours associated with the availability and purchase of repossessed property, as Michelle points out in the quotation above. If you are interested in buying a repossessed house or flat for residential use, it is important that you find out the facts so that you know what is available, how to access information, understand the buying and bidding procedure and obtain the bargain property that you seek. These issues are covered throughout this book.

First, however, it is useful to gain an understanding of what is meant by repossession, why property is repossessed, how many properties are repossessed in the UK, what type of property is available and the condition that it is left in. These issues are discussed in this chapter.

WHAT DOES 'REPOSSESSION' MEAN?

'Repossession' involves the taking back of a property by the lender (or seller) from the borrower (or buyer), usually because of default (the failure to meet a contractual obligation). This may include a failure to make the required payments on time or a breach of the terms of the mortgage agreement, such as subletting the property to tenants without permission from the lender. (In itself, subletting without permission may not justify a possession order, but lenders tend to take a tougher view in cases where a borrower has missed monthly mortgage repayments, and then sublets without permission and pockets the rent money.)

When a mortgage is taken out on a property, the property is pledged as security or 'collateral' for the loan. The borrower usually has to sign a document called a 'legal charge' or 'mortgage deed', which will say that if he does not keep up with the repayments, the property can be repossessed. But the creditor can only do this by following certain procedures and it is not able to use 'unreasonable force' to repossess a home. These possession procedures are described in detail in Chapter 2.

'All home-buyers should be aware that their home could be repossessed because we provide written, detailed information that they must read and sign before they receive their loan. Our company makes sure that this information is very clear.'

Mortgage adviser, Northampton.

Once a property has been repossessed, it is put up for sale, either by an estate agent or at auction, with the proceeds going to the lender. If the amount raised by the sale does not cover the amount borrowed, plus the costs associated with the possession order, the borrower remains liable for the shortfall. This amount can be considerable and may include the following:

- Outstanding capital that was originally borrowed, plus interest.

- Arrears.

- Penalty charges for missed payments.

- Insurance. (This may have to be changed if no one is living in the property. This is because most home insurance policies will not provide cover for buildings that are left unoccupied for a certain number of consecutive days, unless a higher premium is paid.)

- Council Tax for at least six weeks.

- Lender's fees that could include the following:

  - Administration fees.

  - Financial counselling/external debt adviser fees (some lenders will provide this service to try to help the borrower who is facing repossession, but they will charge the borrower for the counselling/advice service – see Chapter 2).

  - Legal action fees.

  - Costs relating to taking possession of the property.

- Costs of essential maintenance while the property is being advertised and sold.

- Auctioneer's or estate agent's fees.

The lender has 12 years (five years in Scotland) in which to seek recovery of any outstanding debts via the courts. This 12-year period begins from the date the borrower first fell into arrears, rather than the date the property was sold as a repossession.

Joint borrowers

If two or more borrowers have purchased the property, the lender will treat them as 'jointly and severally liable' for the entire amount borrowed, irrespective of how much each person paid on a monthly basis or the type of ownership of the property, such as a 'joint tenancy' or 'tenancy in common'. (A joint tenant shares undivided ownership of the property and his share is automatically passed to the other owner on death, whereas a tenant in common owns his share of the property that he can pass to whoever he wishes on his death.)

WHY IS PROPERTY REPOSSESSED?

As I have already mentioned, property is repossessed because a borrower defaults on his loan. This may be for a number of reasons:

- Financial overcommitment and/or mismanagement. The borrower overstretches himself by taking out a loan that he struggles to pay back. Experts and journalists blame mortgage companies for this problem, believing that they are too willing to lend large amounts of money without first checking that the borrower will be able to repay the loan. Low-income borrowers are most at risk of repossession and nearly half of mortgages at risk have loans relative to property values (LTV) of 100 per cent. (See the Glossary of Terms for more information about LTVs.) The term 'sub-prime' mortgage has been used to describe this type of loan, which is typically acquired by borrowers with a poor credit history or no credit history at all. Because the default risk is greater for this type of borrower, lenders charge a higher interest rate on sub-prime loans, and borrowers can find them a struggle to pay back.

- A change in circumstances that leads to loss of income, such as redundancy, illness or becoming a carer, which renders the borrower unable to continue with his mortgage payments. This problem could have been overcome by taking out adequate Mortgage Payment Protection Insurance (MPPI) that protects against unplanned or unexpected changes in circumstances. However, recent research by Shelter, the national charity campaigning on housing and homelessness, suggests that those most at risk of default through loss of income are the least likely to have insurance (www.shelter.org.uk).

- Divorce or separation, resulting in someone being unable to meet his mortgage repayments on his own. But, as we have seen on page 3, both parties will still be liable for the debt if the mortgage was in joint names.

- A rise in interest rates, an eventuality the borrower failed to take into account, or misunderstood the effect of, and the effect this has on the level of mortgage repayments. In other cases, the borrower may have taken out the wrong type of mortgage for the market conditions, either through inadequate research or through taking the wrong advice.

- Taking out a second loan/mortgage and building up other debts. Some borrowers have tried to cover debts or make alterations to their property by taking out a second mortgage or loan, which they then struggle to pay back. Indeed, multiple debts are a common feature of those facing repossession, with many believing that access to secondary credit has been too easy for them.

- Some borrowers rely heavily on the advice of a broker, failing to realise that this person is tied to offering advice about specific products. They believe this advice to be the most appropriate and they do not shop around for alternatives.

The charity Citizens Advice Bureau (CAB) believes that sub-prime lenders are too quick to take court action for relatively small amounts of arrears and are failing to treat customers fairly. They believe that this aggressive approach by lenders to people in arrears is driving an increase in court actions for repossession. This has prompted the Financial Services Authority (FSA) to investigate into the way that lenders deal with people who are in financial difficulty. More information about this action taken by lenders, and the investigation by the FSA, is provided in Chapter 2.

THE SCALE OF REPOSSESSIONS IN THE UK

The Council of Mortgage Lenders (CML) is the trade association for mortgage lenders in the UK. Its membership is made up of banks, building societies and other lenders (www.cml.org.uk). Research conducted by the CML indicates that there were 22,400 mortgage repossessions in 2006 and 27,100 in 2007 and they predict that this number will rise to 45,000 in 2008. The Royal Institution of Chartered Surveyors (RICS) has also suggested that repossessions will continue to climb into 2008 and could exceed 45,000 (www.rics.org).

This figure represents only 0.4 per cent of all home loans in the UK, illustrating that, despite recent increases in repossession figures, the number of repossessions relative to the number of mortgages is still very low. Also, this figure is much less than the number of repossessions experienced in 1991, which totalled 75,540.

'Certainly, we expect the number of people who are having problems meeting mortgage payments to increase over the next few years as the credit crunch begins to bite. I'm old enough to remember what happened in the nineties and I've got a horrible feeling things are going to repeat themselves.'

Mortgage adviser, Northampton.

The CML points out that, at present, there are 11.6 million mortgages in the UK, with loans worth over £1 trillion. Since 1991, there have been an extra 1.9 million mortgages on the market. Due to the market being increasingly competitive, mortgage lenders are keen to attract new customers. One way that they do this is to be positioned top of 'best buy' mortgage tables that appear in newspapers and on internet mortgage comparison sites. These tables list the most attractive mortgage deals in terms of interest rates, but often hide additional charges, such as high arrangement fees, which make the deals less favourable.

Politicians are becoming increasingly concerned about the methods adopted by mortgage lenders to do this, especially when the number of repossessions is increasing. A recent Early Day Motion (EDM) that was submitted for debate in the House of Commons stated the following:

> *'That this House notes with concern the trend of increasing levels of arrangement fees associated with new mortgage products; further notes that high arrangement fees are being used to subsidise low headline interest rates so as to ensure that mortgage products appear in best buy tables, even where such mortgages are not the best buy once account is taken of the fees charged; further notes that in press advertisements the low headline interest rate is given considerable prominence while the high arrangement fee is given less prominence; further notes that these questionable promotional practices occur at a time of growing mortgage arrears, repossessions and repossession orders; is concerned that poorly advised homebuyers may be attracted by such low headline rates which may not be good value for money…and calls on the financial services industry to ensure that all of the key elements of a mortgage deal are given equal prominence and to take other steps to ensure that homebuyers are not sold inappropriate mortgage products.'*

EDM 915, Session 06-07.

More information about EDMs can be obtained from http://edmi.parliament.uk.

In addition to problems associated with inappropriate mortgage products, experts believe that inflated house prices have forced people to borrow more and more money that they cannot afford. RICS produces an 'accessibility index' that shows how much people have to pay for their home and the associated costs, and how this has changed over the years. In 2007, they found that constantly rising house prices have meant that accessibility is around 230 times worse than it was ten years ago. They go on to point out that a typical first-time buyer couple will now have to save up to the equivalent of 82 per cent of their joint income to build up enough to pay for their home and the associated costs. In 1996, this figure was 25 per cent. Even with recent falls in house prices, RICS believes that these problems, which people are currently experiencing with accessibility, will inevitably lead to more repossessions in 2008.

WHAT REPOSSESSED PROPERTIES ARE AVAILABLE?

Repossessions are occurring throughout the UK. But, at the time of writing, we are seeing a significant rise in repossessions in London and the south of England, where many borrowers have overstretched themselves financially because of high house prices in these areas. Elsewhere, there has been a rapid increase in the number of city-centre apartments that have been repossessed, especially in Manchester, Liverpool and Newcastle. This is due, in part, to the number of buy-to-let investors who made unwise investment decisions (see quote below).

 *'We're certainly experiencing more problems here, but our offices in larger cities are also having problems. One in Liverpool springs to mind…My colleague reported a growth in possession orders on city-centre apartments. I can't give any exact figures though, so it's all anecdotal.'*

Mortgage adviser, Northampton.

Although it is possible for all sorts of residential property to be repossessed, there are certain categories that tend to be more widespread. These include the following:

- Local authority and housing association properties that have been bought under the government's Right to Buy scheme (see page 8).

- Properties that have been bought by landlords to let to tenants, which tend to be terraced houses or flats.

- Maisonettes and flats that are only a few years old, which originally were bought by investors from new.

- Guest houses in holiday resorts (sometimes referred to as boarding houses or bed and breakfast accommodation).

Property sold under the Right to Buy scheme

Under the government's Right to Buy scheme, council tenants and some housing association tenants are able to buy their homes, thus becoming homeowners rather than tenants. A tenant who has the right to buy his home is offered a discount on the market value of the property according to the region in which the property is located and the length of time that the tenant, or his spouse, has lived at the property. The discount also depends on whether the property is a house or flat and whether it has been improved recently.

Since the scheme began, more than two million people have become owner-occupiers using this method, according to the charity Shelter. While the majority have successfully bought their homes, others have experienced problems with arrears, and some have lost their homes through repossession. Some of the causes of repossession were given earlier, but there are others that relate specifically to the Right to Buy scheme, which include the following:

- Those with mortgages who experience a fall in income are less entitled to receive public assistance with their housing costs than tenants. Although homeowners who qualify for Income Support or Jobseeker's Allowance are able to receive assistance, rules stipulate that they will not qualify for the first 39 weeks from the date of claiming support if they took out their mortgage after October 1995. Also, if they were claiming benefits before they took out their mortgage, they may not be entitled to receive any financial help at all. Financial assistance will only be given for interest on the mortgage and the amount is based on the average interest rate at the time a claim is made. This may be lower than the actual rate that a homeowner is paying, which means that he has to find the shortfall from elsewhere.

- Tenants may underestimate the costs associated with buying their property. These can include Stamp Duty Land Tax (SDLT), legal costs, conveyancing fees, land registration fees, valuation fees and survey fees. Once they have paid these costs, they struggle to find enough money to meet mortgage payments.

- Tenants may underestimate the costs associated with maintaining a property, including structural repairs, property improvements, service charges, maintenance of drains, sewers and water pipes and insurances costs.

- Tenants failed to obtain a full structural survey of the property, believing that they knew everything about the property at the time of purchase. Unfortunately, they subsequently find out that major structural work is required and they are unable to meet the costs without taking on another loan, which they struggle to pay back.

It is possible to obtain repossessed property that was originally bought under the Right to Buy scheme at a bargain price because some buyers looking for a home are less willing to consider ex-council houses, which results in fewer bids on the property. In some cases, you may be the only person to make an offer on the property and the lender may be willing to accept your offer in the hope of making a quick sale. More information about making an appropriate offer and understanding the bidding procedure is provided in Chapter 8.

'The estate agent told us that there had only been one other offer and that was way below ours. I must admit that it made me wonder whether there was anything wrong with it, but the estate agent said it might be because it was an ex-local authority house. Well, we're not that snobby!'

Email from a purchaser who wishes to remain anonymous, Bournemouth.

But, in some cases, you will need to approach this type of property with caution. For example, some local authority housing constructed in the 1940s and 1950s were built of pre-cast reinforced concrete that are now suffering from, what has been named, 'concrete cancer'. This is a condition that occurs in ageing concrete and is caused by the steel supports within the concrete beginning to rust and react to temperature and water. The concrete deteriorates over time, which eventually causes the structure of the building to weaken.

Some houses were sold to tenants before this problem was recognised, and, if such a property has been repossessed and is offered for sale, the lender is under no obligation to declare the problem to potential purchasers. All residential property that is offered for sale in England and Wales must include a Home Information Pack (HIP), and this could alert you to the fact that the property is of 'non-traditional' construction, which includes those properties built of pre-cast reinforced concrete. (More information about HIPs and the Scottish equivalent, which is being introduced in December 2008, is provided in Chapter 7.) But, since the Home Condition Report (HCR) is a voluntary component of a HIP, it is unlikely that detailed information about structural defects specific to the property will be readily available in the pack, although it may be possible that local searches indicate that there is a recognised problem of this nature in the area (see Chapter 10 for more information about local searches). It is important that you know how to recognise this type of problem, and how to commission a full survey of the property, if you are in doubt. Information about recognising the condition is provided in Chapter 7.

A buyer of a repossessed property on this estate in south Dorset was alerted to the problem of 'concrete cancer' when he commissioned a full survey on the property. The borrower pulled out of the sale as the problem was too expensive to rectify.

Buy-to-let properties

Buy-to-let properties have become increasingly popular over the past decade, with investors believing that there are large profits to be made over both the short and long term. But unwise investment, inadequate research, inexperience and financial mismanagement have led to a rising number of landlords experiencing buy-to-let repossessions. Research by the CML indicates that, although repossessions on buy-to-let mortgages have been consistently lower than homebuyer mortgages, the gap is now narrowing.

With the number of buy-to-let mortgages having risen by 50 per cent in 2006 to 330,000, and with the recent rises in interest rates and falling house prices, it seems inevitable that this type of repossession will increase.

In most cases, a buy-to-let property that is being sold by the lender, as a repossession, will not be tenanted:

'Most tenants have no right to remain in their home once the mortgage lender has been given a possession order by the courts. From this point onwards, anyone living in the property is an 'unlawful occupant' and can be evicted by the bailiffs.'

Shelter, 2008.

But there may be certain cases where the property is still tenanted. This could occur where the tenant was living in the property at the time the mortgage was granted to the landlord. It could also occur in cases where the landlord's lender has specifically recognised the tenancy by, for example, taking rent directly from the tenant. Most lenders, however, will prefer tenants to leave as it is easier for them to dispose of a property that is not tenanted.

This property in Weymouth had been let to tenants but was repossessed in 2000. The tenants had to leave once the lender was granted a possession order by the courts. The present owner bought the property as a repossession in early 2001 for £62,000. Although he was unable to state how much below market value the property was at the time, he knew he had obtained 'a real bargain' because he had been unable to afford any other properties in the area.

Buying a repossessed property to let to tenants

When you are considering buy-to-let properties that have been repossessed, you must think about the reasons for this repossession and make sure that you do not make the same mistakes. Of course, this is the same for any repossessed property, but if you are thinking about a property that you would like to buy so that you can let it to tenants, you must understand why the venture has failed in the past. Questions you will need to consider include:

- Is the location suitable for residential lets?

- Are there tenants available in the area, or, if the property is still tenanted, are you happy to keep on the existing tenants?

- Has saturation point been reached on rental property in the area?

- What rent can you realistically charge? Perhaps surprisingly, rent levels are still rising in some parts of the UK because some smaller buy-to-let investors are selling their properties, which means that more tenants are competing for fewer properties. But this is not the case in all areas, so you will need to conduct thorough research into rent levels before you buy in a specific area.

- Will the amount of rent that you can charge give you a good return on your investment?

If you are new to the buy-to-let market, you should seek professional advice before making your purchase.

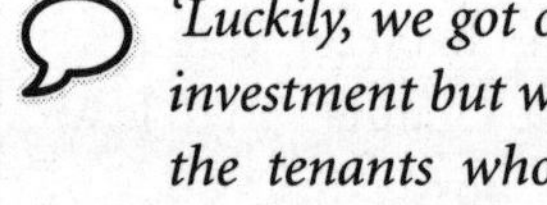

'Luckily, we got out just in time. We'd bought the house as an investment but we paid far too much and we just couldn't find the tenants who were willing to pay the rent we needed. Luckily, we sold before the mortgage people repossessed us. I'd not do that again. I saw all those programmes on the telly and I thought it'd be so easy being a landlord, but it wasn't.'

Sally, Bristol.

Recent new-build properties

Over the past decade, new flats and maisonettes have been built all over the UK as builders and developers cashed in on rising house prices and took advantage of the increasing demand for new-build property of this type. Many of these properties were bought by property investors who were hoping to let the property to tenants and make a good return on their investment. Some were offered for sale with what appeared to be, at the time, a favourable discount on the asking price if potential buyers could move quickly on the sale.

But some property investors and landlords found that they were unable to find tenants for the flats and maisonettes, or they were unable to charge enough rent to cover mortgage payments on their buy-to-let mortgage. Unfortunately, falling house prices meant that they could not pull out of the investment because they would have to sell the property for less than they had originally paid, even when the discount on the original selling price was taken into account. This situation – being unable to cover mortgage payments, yet being unable to sell – has led to a number of repossessions of these types of flat and maisonette that have been built within the past ten years or so.

At least two flats in this complex in south Dorset were repossessed in 2007. This development was completed in stages over a two-year period from 2003. Discounts were offered to investors who bought more than one apartment, but landlords have been unable to receive enough income from letting out the flats. The estate agent dealing with the sale of flats in this complex would not tell me which of the flats had been repossessed, nor whether they had been sold. But he did point out that there were now three flats for sale (July 2008) and that all three were being offered at ten to 15 per cent below the current market value. He seemed to be suggesting that all three flats were repossessions and that they provided a good bargain for people interested in this type of property.

In some cases, property investors bought a number of flats within the same newly built complex, as they were offered a discount if they did so. Unfortunately, this meant that a few years down the line a number of flats within the same complex were repossessed, often by the same lender. When a number of flats are offered for sale at the same time in the same complex, prices are pushed down. As a potential purchaser you have more scope to make a low offer on this type of repossessed property as the lender will need to make a quick sale, especially if it is trying to dispose of more than one property within the complex. Also, if your low offer is not accepted on one flat, you may have scope to make a low offer on another repossessed flat within the same complex. Where one lender is unwilling to accept your low offer, another may be willing to do so.

Guest houses

Part of the research for this book took place on the south coast of England. In seaside resorts along this coast there are a large number of guest houses (also referred to as boarding houses or bed and breakfast accommodation). These tend to be terraced, semi-detached or detached properties, containing up to ten bedrooms that are let to holidaymakers, usually on a daily or weekly tariff. My research has found that the number of guest houses that are being repossessed is increasing in this part of the UK. This could be for a number of reasons:

- The English weather is unpredictable. The summer of 2007 in the UK was the wettest since records began, according to the Met Office. Many holidaymakers chose to go abroad for their holidays and UK guest house owners could not fill their accommodation. Some were unable to meet mortgage payments as a result.

- Some people take on ownership of guest houses with little knowledge or research, and with unrealistic expectations about income and expenditure. They are unable to receive enough income to cover their mortgage payments.

- Media coverage of the credit crunch and fear about a possible recession has resulted in people saving money and taking fewer holidays. Again, UK guest house owners are unable to fill their accommodation and they find that they are getting into debt.

Some of the larger guest houses that have been repossessed due to the problems described above have been snapped up by property developers who are converting them into separate flats. For example, a seven-bedroom guest house in my local town that had been repossessed was bought by a property developer. He is in the process of converting the property into three flats, one with three bedrooms, one with two bedrooms and one with one bedroom. He intends to sell the flats once they are completed (see the picture on page 15).

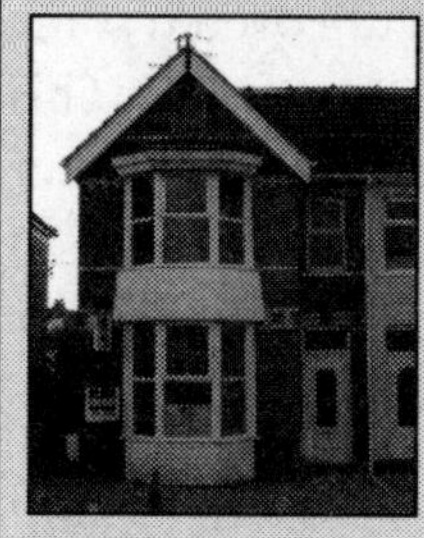

This property used to be a guest house and is located in Weymouth. It was bought in 2007 for £273,000 after repossession, at around ten per cent cheaper than the market price. It is being converted into three flats by a local property developer.

Some of the smaller guest houses that are repossessed are suitable as family homes and, because property developers tend to prefer larger buildings that can be converted, you may not have to compete against these developers when you are making your bid.

Buying a property to run as a guest house

If you are hoping to buy a repossessed guest house to run as a business, you must try to find out why the venture has failed in the past, so that you do not make the same mistakes. Although you will not be able to obtain confidential information specific to the property in which you are interested, you should be able to obtain general information about the performance of the tourism market from the local tourist information office, local authority and local guest house association.

WHAT CONDITION ARE PROPERTIES IN?

Losing your home is an incredibly distressing event and people react in different ways. Some leave their property in a good state of repair. They understand that the lender needs to obtain the best price possible for the property so that they, as the evicted borrower, can clear their debts. Others, however, react angrily, believing that they have been treated unfairly by the lender. As they are so angry, they damage their property before they leave, sometimes stripping it of fixtures and fittings, and sometimes causing malicious damage for the next occupant.

Because every case is different, it is difficult to say what condition repossessed properties will be in – this is something that you will need to find out when you view a property – but my research has uncovered some serious problems with the way that some properties have been left. This includes people leaving live wires exposed and pins inserted into water cylinders. As a potential purchaser, it is important that you are aware of these issues and that you know how to spot potential problems. These issues are discussed in detail in Chapters 7 and 11.

SUMMARY

Repossession involves the taking back of a property by the lender from the borrower, usually because of default. Once a property has been repossessed, it is sold through an estate agent or at auction, with the proceeds going to the lender. All sorts of properties have the potential to be repossessed, but there are certain types of property that more commonly occur as repossessions, such as ex-council housing that has been bought under the Right to Buy scheme or properties that were bought by landlords to let to tenants. On the south coast of England there are an increasing number of guest houses that are being repossessed. It is predicted that the number of repossessions in the UK will reach 45,000 in 2008. This is due, in part, to financial problems associated with the credit crunch and due to problems with borrowers overstretching themselves financially.

If you are interested in purchasing a repossessed property, it is useful to understand the repossession procedures that are adopted by mortgage lenders so that you can understand when and how to enter the purchasing process. These issues are discussed in the following chapter.

CHAPTER 2:

UNDERSTANDING THE REPOSSESSION PROCEDURE

 *'It's actually quite a complicated procedure and we obviously don't want to take someone's home if there's something we can do about it. There is a set procedure we're asked to follow, but, obviously, all cases are different and we treat everyone individually. We have to move through this procedure before properties appear on the market and if we go to court, we've got to follow the law…it's useful for people who are thinking about buying this kind of property to understand the procedure.'*

Mortgage adviser, Northampton.

When borrowers find themselves struggling to repay their loan, some mortgage lenders tend to be flexible and treat each case individually, as highlighted in the quotation above. Others, however, are much more rigid in their approach and some experts believe that they are not treating customers fairly (see page 18).

All lenders are required to follow a set of procedures if a property is likely to be repossessed through the courts. If you are interested in buying repossessed property, it is useful to gain an awareness of these procedures so that you can understand at what stage a property becomes available on the market, and so you know about the problems that could arise if you decide to purchase this type of property. These procedures are discussed in this chapter.

MORTGAGE ARREARS

When a borrower defaults on his mortgage payments, or mortgage payments are overdue, he is said to be 'in arrears'. Often, the first indication received by a lender that a borrower has financial difficulties is that monthly payments are missed or late. This is because some borrowers are worried about admitting that they are in financial trouble, whereas others choose to bury their heads in the sand and refuse to disclose that they are experiencing problems. Whatever the reasons, as soon as payments are missed, lenders attempt to recover the arrears.

The policy for recovering arrears

When a lender is seeking to recover arrears, it should comply with the standards set by the Financial Services Authority (FSA) under the Mortgage Conduct of Business (www.moneymadeclear.fsa.gov.uk). All customers should be treated fairly and the lender should have a clear, written policy for dealing with customers who find themselves in arrears. The lender should try to negotiate a new repayment plan that is tailored to the borrower's needs and circumstances.

Recently, however, the FSA has expressed concern that lenders are not treating customers fairly and on an individual basis. In 2008 it is inspecting the approach of up to 12 major lenders and those that have breached the rules over arrears could face fines, public sanctions or a ban on conducting further business. The FSA is concerned that the situation could get worse in the UK with the number of repossessions set to rise in 2008 and with the fallout from the US sub-prime mortgage crisis and the subsequent credit crunch. Indeed, the FSA predicts that nearly one-fifth of those who took out a mortgage between April 2005 and September 2007 risk having their property repossessed, if current trends continue.

Guidelines for developing a payment plan

In line with FSA guidelines, most lenders ask that borrowers inform them immediately if they are struggling to make payments, but if this does not happen, the lender should contact the borrower to find out why payment has stopped. Once contact has been made, both parties should try to come to a satisfactory agreement, developing a payment plan that is feasible and realistic.

'You'd be surprised how many people don't tell us that they've got problems paying [the mortgage]. But if they told us, we'd be able to help much quicker and they probably wouldn't find themselves in so much debt because we have payment plans and things that can help.'

Mortgage adviser, Northampton.

Some lenders may require a meeting to take place with a specialist financial adviser in the borrower's own home and they will make a charge for their services, usually in the region of £100–£150. In addition to working out a payment plan, good financial advisers will raise awareness of alternative sources of income, such as social security benefits for borrowers who are unemployed. They should direct borrowers to independent sources of free financial advice, such as Citizens Advice Bureaux (www.citizensadvice. org.uk) and the Consumer Credit Counselling Service (www.cccs.co.uk). Also, the financial adviser should provide the borrower with the FSA leaflet 'What to do when you can't meet your mortgage payments'.

In most cases, lenders will refer arrears accounts to their specialist departments or members of staff who will monitor the account to make sure that the borrower is adhering to the plan. A record of the mortgage arrears may be held by a credit reference agency. This is an organisation that has been set up to collect and store information on a person's financial position in order to provide factual information to financial organisations, when requested. More information about credit reference agencies is provided in Chapters 4 and 12.

ALLEVIATING ARREARS PROBLEMS

According to the Council of Mortgage Lenders (CML), most lenders are keen to sort out problems with their clients before they escalate. Methods adopted to recover arrears depend on the type of mortgage and individual circumstances, but they may include the following:

- **Deferment of interest.** This method is useful for borrowers who are experiencing a temporary shortfall of income because of illness, for example, or an industrial dispute. Once the temporary problem is resolved, the borrower can make up the shortfall.

- **Consolidation.** If a borrower is in danger of losing his home, he may be advised to borrow more money to pay priority debts. But this strategy should be approached with caution as borrowing more money may not be the best solution for those in financial difficulty.

- **Payment holiday.** Some lenders are willing to enable borrowers who have a more 'flexible' mortgage to take a break from their mortgage repayments, if they are able to show that they can make up the shortfall after a specified period of time.

- **An extension of the term of the mortgage.** This may be an option for borrowers who have a repayment mortgage. Although the amount of monthly repayment is not reduced significantly, it may help those experiencing a small shortfall.

- **A reduction of the payments.** This can be done by changing the type of mortgage and it may significantly reduce the monthly bill, especially for those who have not reviewed their mortgage arrangements for some time.

- **Put arrears on hold but request normal payments.** This is an arrangement that may help some borrowers to sort out their finances over the short term. The amount outstanding can be rescheduled and repaid over the life of the loan.

- **An arrangement for payment of interest only.** Again, this may help borrowers to sort out their finances over the short term.

- **Ask for normal payments, plus extra to cover the arrears.** This option is used if a detailed plan indicates that the borrower is able to meet the payments through careful planning and saving.

Through adopting one or more of the above methods, many borrowers, who are experiencing minor arrears, are able to overcome the shortfall and resume their payment plan. But if the problem is not resolved, the Court of Appeal has held that a lender has a common law right to take possession of a property peaceably without first obtaining a court order. This situation tends to arise when a property has been abandoned or surrendered (see below).

METHODS OF OBTAINING POSSESSION

Lenders should obtain possession only as a last resort, when all other payment plans have failed and the borrower is unable to continue repaying his loan, according to the FSA. In most cases, this will be when arrears have remained unpaid for two to six months, or more, depending on the practices of the lender. Lenders are able to repossess property in the three ways, described below.

Voluntary agreement

Some borrowers realise that they are unable to continue to repay the loan and, after discussion with financial advisers or the lender, agree to hand over the keys to their property. In these cases the lender does not have to go to court and, in theory, it should help to speed up the sale of the property. The borrower should be asked to sign a 'voluntary possession declaration' to confirm that he has agreed to the decision and that he understands that he is still liable for all mortgage payments and costs until the property is sold.

In general, this type of agreement tends to be the most amicable arrangement. My research seems to suggest that these properties are less likely to be damaged or stripped and there are fewer problems with debt collectors and bad credit. As a quick sale benefits both parties, the property should be advertised quickly with a realistic but reasonable sale or guide price (see Chapter 4).

Surrender or abandonment

In some cases, the borrower is unwilling to discuss his financial problems with the lender and, after having missed a number of repayments, abandons his property, either by sending the keys to the lender without discussion ('surrender'), or by moving out without notifying the mortgage company ('abandonment'). In these cases, it can take the lender some time to establish that the property has been abandoned and this will delay the time it takes for the property to reach the market.

When a borrower enters into a mortgage arrangement, he makes an agreement that the mortgage company has the right to 'enter into possession' of the property if the terms of the agreement are breached. In cases of abandonment, the terms are deemed to have been breached if at least two months of payments have been missed, a notice requiring payment has been ignored, and when a further three or more months of payments have been missed and the borrower cannot be contacted at the mortgaged address. It is at this stage that the lender will be able to 'exercise the powers of sale'. But although the property can be sold, this does not mean there has been a change in ownership – the borrower is still legally the owner and is responsible for any outstanding debt or will receive any profit realised from the sale (see Chapter 10).

Anecdotal evidence suggests that it is this type of abandoned property that is more likely to be damaged or stripped of fittings and fixtures, as illustrated in the quotation below:

> *'Certainly it is hard to know sometimes when someone has gone. Some of them go and leave everything, but a lot go and take everything with them. And I mean everything. You wouldn't believe what some people can take from a property. In one place there were no light switches, fittings and bulbs; they'd even managed to pull the wires from the walls and all the radiators, pipes and boiler had gone, even the fence from the garden. Sometimes they have more time, you know, if we don't know that they're going to disappear and then they leave the house as an empty shell. It's quite incredible really.'*

Mortgage adviser, Northampton.

As a potential purchaser of this type of property, you would have to undertake a careful and detailed viewing, checking that all door and window locks have been changed and ensuring that the property is safe. Information and advice about viewing a property and obtaining safety checks is provided in Chapters 7 and 11. You also need to make sure that an appropriate survey is arranged (see Chapter 7) and you must make sure that your solicitor or conveyancer undertakes a thorough investigation of title and ownership and carries out the appropriate searches (see Chapter 10).

Court order

In cases where a lender is unable to recover arrears and if the property has not been surrendered or abandoned, it may decide to go to court to gain a possession order. If a lender decides to initiate court proceedings, it must adhere to all the legal procedures and requirements. This includes the following steps:

- **Stage 1.** The lender sends a standard letter asking that missed payments are paid or that the borrower contacts the lender to discuss the issue.

- **Stage 2.** If a satisfactory arrangement has not been made, and the borrower is in arrears of at least two months, the lender sends a letter requiring action in seven days, or the lender's solicitor will become involved.

- **Stage 3.** If the problem is not resolved or the borrower does not contact the lender within seven days, a letter from the lender's solicitor is sent asking that the arrears be cleared or a suitable payment plan put in place. Again, the borrower must respond within seven days and if this does not happen, possession proceedings will be started without further notice.

- **Stage 4.** Approximately four to six weeks after the solicitor's letter is sent, the County Court issues a claim for possession of the property. The lender must also send a letter to the borrower stating that possession proceedings have started, at least 14 days before the possession hearing.

- **Stage 5.** The possession hearing takes place. The judge can decide on the following courses of action:

  - Dismiss the case if it is felt that the correct procedures have not been followed or the lender does not have a case.

  - Adjourn the case if, for example, it is felt that the borrower is able to repay the money in a reasonable time frame or if the borrower has found a buyer and needs to be given more time to sell the property himself to avoid repossession.

- Make a suspended possession order whereby the borrower must agree to certain conditions, such as making certain payments towards his arrears. If these conditions are breached, the lender can apply to the court immediately for a 'warrant of possession'.

- Make a time order if, for example, the judge feels that the borrower should be given more time to repay a debt. A borrower can apply to a County Court for a time order before possession proceedings begin, although this option is available only where a mortgage is secured under the Consumer Credit Act 1974.

- Make a money judgment, whereby a lender is able to recover the total sum due, including arrears and all other costs. A money judgment can be attached to a possession order, which means that someone loses his home and has to pay arrears.

- Make an outright possession order. If this is the case, the court will give a date by which the property must become vacant, which is usually 28 days, although, in certain circumstances, it could be up to six weeks.

- **Stage 6.** The bailiffs make sure that the borrower understands the date and time of the eviction and ensure that the property is vacated at this time. They are able to use 'necessary force' to enter the property but they cannot use 'unreasonable force' to evict borrowers, and they will change the locks on the day of eviction. All belongings must be removed within a short period of time, by agreement with the lender. If this does not happen, the lender is entitled to dispose of them, prior to the sale of the property.

STOPPING A REPOSSESSED PROPERTY FROM BEING SOLD

As a potential purchaser, you should understand that, in certain circumstances, a borrower who is facing eviction, or who has already been evicted, may be able to stop the sale of his home from going ahead. This could happen in the following circumstances:

- If the correct legal process was not followed by the lender or its solicitor.

- If the borrower is able to raise the money to pay off his mortgage debt soon after the eviction, he could apply for an injunction to stop the sale of his home.

- If there has been an 'abuse of process' or 'oppressive conduct' in the execution of the warrant by the court bailiffs.

- If the borrower can prove that the property has been undervalued, he can ask the courts for an injunction to prevent a sale.

- If the borrower can prove that he can sell the property for a better price than the lender, he can apply for an order of sale. This prevents the lender from selling the property for a limited amount of time.

This means that, if you are attempting to buy a property that has been repossessed, there is a possibility that the owner could stop the sale and regain ownership, or sell the property to someone else for a higher price. But if you have already exchanged contracts on the property, an evicted borrower cannot stop the sale or sell to someone else (see Chapter 10).

Losing a home is an extremely traumatic experience – if you are in the process of buying a repossessed property and the previous owner tries to regain ownership, you will have to make a decision about the best course of action. You may decide that it is better to walk away from the sale and enable someone to return to his home, rather than fight for the property. This is a matter of personal conscience and will be influenced by your personal circumstances and that of the evictee (see Chapters 4 and 11).

SUMMARY

If you are hoping to buy a repossessed property, it is important to understand the repossession procedure as this will help you to know when and how properties appear on the market. In particular, it is important to understand the different ways in which properties are repossessed as this has implications for the speed at which they can be placed on the market and the problems that could occur for you with borrowers attempting to reclaim their home. The ways that properties are repossessed are through voluntary agreement, through surrender or abandonment, or through court proceedings. Voluntary agreement usually means that the property is placed on the market quickly, whereas following correct legal procedures and obtaining a possession order can take several months. A person who has lost his home through repossession can try to stop the sale right up until the exchange of contracts.

The next part of the process is the disposal procedure through which properties that have been repossessed are marketed and advertised. These issues are discussed in the following chapter.

CHAPTER 3:

UNDERSTANDING THE DISPOSAL PROCEDURE

> *'There was a house next door to us which had been repossessed. Well, I'm pretty sure it had been repossessed because the people who lived there did a runner and then eventually it came up on the market at an auction. But how did that happen? I wanted to found out how much it went for, obviously because it would give us an idea of how much ours was worth, but I couldn't find out and then some property developer bought the house and then it went back on the market really quickly. He seemed to be in the know. How did that happen?'*

Jim, Northampton.

During my research into buying repossessed property, several people pointed out that they did not understand how properties that had been repossessed appeared on the market. They felt that it was confusing and difficult for individual people to find out about available properties and it appeared that property developers were the only people 'in the know', as illustrated in the quotation above.

If you are interested in buying a repossessed property, it is useful to understand the disposal procedure so that you can gain an awareness of how repossessed properties are valued, how they appear on the market, who maintains and looks after the property while it is for sale, and what happens to the proceeds once a sale is completed. These issues are discussed in this chapter.

VALUING THE PROPERTY

The Financial Ombudsman Service (FOS) advises that a lender who has repossessed a property should obtain at least two valuations for the property, one of which should be independent (www.financial-ombudsman.org.uk). Valuations should be reviewed every three to four months or if circumstances change and they justify a revaluation of the property, such as a sudden rise or fall in property prices in the area.

It is recommended that valuations are undertaken by both a surveyor and an estate agent. The evicted borrower can contact the lender to find out whether these valuations have taken place to make sure that the lender is attempting to obtain the best price for his property. If an evicted borrower believes that a property has been undervalued, he can go to court to ask for an injunction to prevent the sale. If he is successful, the courts may make an order allowing the evicted borrower to sell the property himself (an order for sale).

In most cases an evicted borrower will have to pay court and legal advice fees, which may deter some people taking this course of action. But evicted borrowers, who are on low incomes or benefits, may have their costs paid for them and all borrowers can receive free legal advice from their Citizens Advice Bureau (CAB). Also, the Prevention of Homelessness Act 2004 enables the courts to waiver fees and charges where they consider it reasonable to do so in order to prevent homelessness.

An injunction to prevent the sale can be done at any time before the exchange of contracts between the lender and the new buyer (see Case Study 1 on page 36). Also, borrowers may be entitled to compensation if the lender has not sold the property at a fair and reasonable price (see page 29).

'Our neighbour left her house on her own accord. Then it was put up for sale and she wasn't happy with the price. I wouldn't have been either. It was far too cheap. You would think they would know how much it should be worth, wouldn't you? My

*husband said it was to get more punters looking at it. But it
didn't sell for ages. It makes you wonder, doesn't it?'*

A neighbour of a property located in Plymouth.

But, in practice, many repossessed properties are offered at auction, which often means that they can sell below the usual market price for that type of property. Others are offered through estate agents who have been instructed to consider a lower offer if a quick sale can be achieved. This could occur, for example, when the potential buyer already has a mortgage in place and is not part of a chain. Also, some estate agents have been known to work closely with local property developers, offering the property at a cheaper price for a 'cash finder's fee' so that they can secure a quick sale. While this practice is unethical and could, in some cases, be unlawful, it appears that some lenders turn a blind eye because they need to dispose of the property to regain their money as quickly as possible. This practice could be unlawful because estate agents, by law, should not accept secret commissions, discounts, rebates or other profits from any person in connection with the affairs of a client, unless the details have been disclosed to the client. More information about this practice is provided in Chapter 8.

*'I shouldn't be telling you this because you will let the cat out
of the bag, but, of course, it happens. It's well worth it for me.
I give them cash up front and they let me have first dibs on a
property. It saves me time and it saves them time. And really
it's got to be good for the person who's left because they sell
their house quickly. Well, the mortgage company sells it quickly
and gets its money back. No, I don't have a problem with it.
OK, it might not be very legal, but you're not going to print my
name or address anyway, are you?*

An anonymous property investor, location not specified.

Selling a property too cheaply

If a property sells at a price that is well below the valuation price, in theory, it is possible for the borrower to sue the lender for negligence. This is because the lender is under a legal obligation to obtain the best price for the property that can be reasonably obtained. A borrower would have to prove that the lender has not done this by obtaining independent valuations, in writing, for his property and proving that the price was not 'reasonable'. But, in practice it is rare that an evicted borrower would sue a lender because of the costs involved, unless he is able to get his fees waivered (see page 28).

Also, in theory, it could be possible for a lender to make a claim for negligence against an estate agent if the estate agent has accepted a lower price without consulting the lender. This is one reason why estate agents and lenders are reluctant to advertise a property as repossessed – they feel that potential buyers will be less willing to pay the full market value for a property that they know to be repossessed, and if they accept a low offer, they could be at risk of being sued. But when this is weighed against the need to make a quick sale, estate agents and lenders are willing to negotiate with potential purchasers, as long as the price is not too low. This is sometimes referred to as a 'forced sale value' of the property, which will be lower than the actual market value of the property.

Mitigating loss

The lender also has a duty to 'mitigate loss', which means that, in addition to obtaining the best price possible, it should make sure that the borrower does not suffer undue loss while the house is being sold. Therefore, the lender must either let the property for a fair market rent or explain why it has decided not to do this. If a borrower believes that his debt has increased due to negligence by the lender while his house is on the market, he could take the lender to court, or make a counter-claim if a lender takes action to recover the rest of the debt. Again, some borrowers may be deterred from this course of action because of the costs involved, although those on low incomes or benefits may have their costs paid for them.

Lenders prefer not to have to maintain a property, secure it against squatters and vandals and find tenants, especially when house prices are falling. This is why some may turn a blind eye to unethical practices by estate agents. Indeed, it has been suggested, during the research for this book, that some lenders have been known to encourage this practice so that they can secure a quick sale. This may be beneficial for property investors and developers, but it puts the ordinary buyer at a disadvantage. Therefore, as an ordinary buyer, it is important that you recognise and, perhaps even, adopt some of the practices utilised by property developers if you are to be successful in your purchase. More information about how to do this is provided in Chapters 8 and 9.

USING ESTATE AGENTS

Many lenders have a close business relationship with local estate agents whom they ask to market, advertise and sell their repossessed properties. In most cases, estate agents are asked specifically not to mention that these properties are repossessed, partly due to the reason outlined above but also because some potential buyers are not keen to buy a repossessed property. This may be due to ethical or moral reasons, or through negative perceptions about the condition of the property and problems that may be encountered with previous owners and debt collectors.

Not advertising that a property is a repossession can make it difficult for individual buyers to obtain information about repossessed properties, although there are ways to overcome this problem, such as recognising the signs of repossession and building up a close relationship with a local estate agent. More information about finding out about repossessions is provided in Chapter 5.

As I have said above, lenders should make sure that estate agents make every effort to sell the property at or above the valuation price. To do this, estate agents will adopt their usual strategies, which could include advertising in the local press, sending out mailshots and advertising nationally or on their website. Estate agents are required to report back to the lender if the property remains unsold for a specific period of time so that the lender can decide whether an alternative course of action is required, such as selling the property at auction.

Receiving offers

If offers are received on the property, the lender is notified, but decisions on whether to accept an offer are usually left to the estate agent, unless the offer is significantly lower than the asking price. In these cases, if an estate agent believes an offer should be accepted, he needs to justify this decision to the lender. But, in practice, some lenders are happy to allow the estate agent to take full control of the sale and this enables some unethical practices to take place. These are described in detail in Chapter 8.

In cases where there are a number of offers on the property, it may go to a sealed bidding process, whereby all bids from interested parties are invited by a certain date, but bidders do not know how much others have bid on the property. When this procedure is used, several potential purchasers have reported problems and suspected 'shady dealings', such as estate agents making bids to increase the offer, and then allowing potential purchasers to raise their bid, even after the closing date for sealed bids. To avoid these problems, you need to make sure that you understand the process and monitor what is happening with your bid. Detailed information about how to do this is provided in Chapters 5 and 8.

'I can't say categorically that it happened, but I'm pretty sure that the estate agent told me a higher offer had been made when I really don't think it had. I should have done something about it, but I just didn't know my rights and what I could do.'

Angela, Southampton.

As a prospective purchaser, you will be accompanied by the estate agent when you are viewing the property, so you need to make sure that you have conducted comprehensive research beforehand and that you have developed a useful checklist and list of questions to ask during the viewing. More information about how to do this is provided in Chapters 6 and 7.

SELLING AT AUCTION

Repossessed properties may be sold at auction for several reasons:

- Estate agents have been unable to sell the property over a set period of time and the lender believes that the property may sell better at auction.

- An auction is targeted specifically at the type of property that is being sold and it is felt that the property would sell well at this type of auction.

- The property will appeal to property investors, developers or speculators who are more likely to buy at auction.

A guide or reserve price is set, depending on the valuation of a surveyor and the amount of interest shown in the property. A catalogue is issued and viewings can take place, usually on set dates up until the time of auction. 'By order of mortgagees' is the term that tends to be used to describe the sale of a repossessed property and it can be used in auction catalogues and during the sale, although some lenders will ask that the auctioneer does not indicate that the property is a repossession. As a potential buyer, you must make sure that all surveys, searches and legal aspects are sorted out before the day of the auction. More information about doing this and the procedures that are adopted at auction is provided in Chapter 9.

'Unfortunately, for their previous owner-occupiers, this category of property continues to feature considerably in many auctioneers' catalogues in the waves of repossessions that occur from time to time. While feeling for those that have been dispossessed, there is no doubt that auction houses, speculators, builders and new-owner occupiers all benefit from such situations. The losses registered by the finance houses and the insurers may only be the result of a drastic domestic property revaluation or may also have been occasioned by the surfeit of vacant houses offered in the sale rooms because of a high level of repossessions at any one time. But there is no doubt that there are some very good value-for-money properties to be purchased at auction. 'Repossession' is not to be considered synonymous with 'bargain'. You should still thoroughly research your target property.'

'Buying Bargains at Property Auctions', Howard R Gooddie. (This book is available from www.lawpack.co.uk.)

MAINTAINING THE PROPERTY

If a property is to be sold through an estate agent, the lender should make sure that all necessary repairs and general maintenance have been undertaken before the property is taken on by the estate agent. But some lenders undertake this task much more diligently than others, with many properties appearing on the market without the required repairs and maintenance. Indeed, my research has illustrated that it is possible for some to be sold in a dangerous and unsafe condition (see Case Study 6, Chapter 11).

The estate agent should then make sure that minor repairs are undertaken during the time that the property remains on the market, although, again, some estate agents are much more diligent than others in this task. Any other work that is required will need approval from the lender and the estate agent is required to make sure that he obtains competitive estimates for the work, as the borrower has to meet these costs. But, in practice, many estate agents work with a particular property maintenance company or have their own department that undertakes this task, and therefore they do not obtain alternative quotations.

Properties that are to be auctioned should be maintained by the lender, who should pay regular visits to make sure that repairs and maintenance are carried out when required. Lenders are obliged to make sure that they obtain the best prices for work that is needed, although, again, in practice, this does not always happen. The borrower is ultimately responsible for paying maintenance and repair costs while the property is being sold and he could, in theory, complain if costs are seen to be excessive. Again, in practice, some lenders are more conscientious than others. My research has shown that some repossessed properties are offered in a dilapidated state because lenders believe that they will be taken on by property developers. As a potential purchaser, you must make sure that you are able to cope with, and afford, any work that is required on the property before you make a bid.

Tenanted properties

As I have mentioned previously, some properties may be tenanted so that an income can be received while the property is on the market, or because an existing tenant has not been evicted. In these cases, it will be the lender, rather than the evicted borrower, who is acting as the landlord and the rent will be paid direct to the lender. If the property has a tenant, you will need to find out for how long his contract runs and make sure that there will be vacant possession upon completion, unless you are happy to continue with the same tenant. This information will be available from the selling agent or lender.

If you prefer to wait until there is vacant possession, this could delay the purchase process, depending on the time left on the tenant's contract, although most lenders will make sure that letting the property does not have a detrimental influence on their ability to make a quick sale. Lenders have to follow the correct possession procedure for assured shorthold tenancies (short assured tenancies in Scotland) and they cannot evict tenants before their contract expires, unless they have a specific legal reason for doing so. Also, you should realise that any other purchaser is able to make a bid on the property right up until the exchange of contracts, so the longer you delay the purchase, the more chance there is that you could lose the property (see Chapter 8 for more information about the bidding procedure). If a property is being offered through auction, it is less likely to be tenanted because the sales process, in general, is much quicker (see Chapter 9).

PROCEEDS AND RECOVERY PROCEDURES

Once a repossessed property has been sold, the lender takes what it is owed from the proceeds of the sale. Estate agent's or auctioneer's fees, any costs for maintenance and repairs that have accrued while the property was on the market and administrative fees are also deducted. Once these costs have been taken off the proceeds, any other loans that have been secured against the property, such as a second mortgage, are repaid. If there is any money left over, it is paid to the borrower. Debts that are owed but that were not secured on the property are a separate matter and creditors have to take separate court action to recover these debts.

In cases where the proceeds of the sale are not enough to cover the debt, the borrower is still liable to repay the outstanding amount. This may occur when there is negative equity on the property or where the property has been sold for less than its market value. If the court did not make a money judgment (described in Chapter 2) during the possession order, in general, the lender will have 12 years in which to recover the outstanding debt (if the loan was secured on the property) and six years (if the loan was not secured on the property). But the Council of Mortgage Lenders (CML) expects its members to start action to recover the debt within six years.

CASE STUDY 1: MARK

Mark is a successful property developer, owning 33 properties that range from one-bedroom flats to seven-bedroom houses. The annual gross rents received by his company in 2007 totalled £317,200. The properties are valued at £3.68 million and Mark has outstanding loans of £2 million.

As a successful property developer, Mark buys houses cheaply and has a list of reliable builders and tradespeople whom he can call upon to work effectively and efficiently on the properties, so that they can be turned around quickly and let to tenants.

Mark has a 'special relationship' with estate agents in his city. He says that he has worked hard to get to know the owners or managers of local estate agents, taking them out for meals, playing golf, socialising and networking. Through building up this type of relationship over a number of years, he has been able to obtain details of many properties before they are advertised, enabling him to make 'reasonable' offers that are often quickly accepted.

A number of these properties have been repossessions and most have been bought easily without any problems. But, in 2005, Mark made an offer on a repossessed, four-bedroom, terraced property through one of his local estate agents. Prices were rising rapidly in the area and Mark knew that he had received an 'exceptional' bargain through his close contact with the estate agent. He made all the usual arrangements, paying legal fees, arranging for searches and paying for a full structural survey, in addition to sorting out a mortgage on the property.

The process was moving smoothly until his solicitor contacted him one morning, explaining that an injunction stopping the sale had been taken out by the evicted owner of the property, who believed that the estate agent had accepted a price well below the current valuation of the property. The evicted owner had found another buyer who was willing to pay a much higher price and the court ruled that the owner should be given the opportunity to sell the property privately (an order for sale), if he could achieve this within a certain time frame.

Mark had to put the purchase of the property on hold. He felt that he would still be able to go ahead with the purchase because he knew that many offers on properties in the area fell through, usually because of problems with the survey, or because of chains breaking down or moving too slowly. Unfortunately for Mark, this sale did go ahead as the purchaser was a cash buyer and not part of a chain.

Although Mark has lost out financially because he had already paid legal costs, surveyor's fees and mortgage administration fees, he was not too upset that he lost the property because he knew that there would be others in the area that he could buy. But he did point out that it would be much worse for a buyer who had set his heart on the property, or who was struggling financially to meet the costs associated with buying a house. There is no refund on these costs and they would all have to be paid again when another suitable property was found.

Mark felt that this experience would not deter him, personally, from buying other repossessed properties, but he did feel that people who were buying this type of property for their main home should be a little more wary. His advice to prospective purchasers is to approach this type of property with caution; if a property seems to be a real bargain, try to find out more about its history from the estate agent. Although some will not disclose private and confidential information, others will, especially if you speak to them 'off the record'. Try to build up a good relationship with the estate agent – be honest and upfront and, hopefully, he will do the same.

SUMMARY

- Properties that have been repossessed are valued and then placed on the market, either through an estate agent or through auction.

- Lenders have a 'duty of care' towards the borrower and should try to obtain the best price possible for the property.

- If a borrower believes that this has not been done, he can take the lender to court, or make a counter-claim. In practice, however, most lenders want to make a quick sale and are willing to negotiate on the price.

- This need for a quick sale has led to a number of 'questionable practices', especially between estate agents and property developers.

- The lender and estate agent are responsible for making sure that the property is well-maintained while it is being sold, although the borrower is responsible for meeting maintenance costs. Despite this, some repossessed properties are sold in a poor state of repair.

Once you understand the repossession and disposal procedure, it is important to recognise the advantages and disadvantages associated with buying repossessed property, so that you can assess whether this type of purchase is the most suitable for your circumstances. These issues are discussed in the following chapter.

CHAPTER 4:

RECOGNISING THE ADVANTAGES AND DISADVANTAGES

'It used to be a guest house and I'd had my eye on it for a while. It used to have naughty kids in it, and I don't know what happened, but next thing I knew they'd all been kicked out, the locks on the door were changed and a notice on the door said that if anyone needed to get into the property for any of their belongings, they should ring a number on the notice. So I knew it had been repossessed. I rang the number and they put me in touch with the mortgage people who told me to get in touch with the estate agent and I took it from there really. There hadn't been a sign up, but it had been for sale for a while, so I know I got a real bargain. I know I did. I don't think that would have happened if it wasn't repossessed. I did feel sorry for the kids though. I don't know where they went.'

Roger, guest house owner, south of England.

In the quotation above, Roger highlights the main advantage of buying repossessed property, which is the price. He also discusses one of the main disadvantages, which is dealing with the fact that you are buying a property from which people have been evicted. Although it is not explicitly mentioned, Roger also hints at another advantage of buying repossessed property, which is the house-buying process can run much quicker if all parties wish to make a quick sale, as there is no chain involved with the house being purchased. Additional disadvantages not mentioned by Roger could include damage and problems with debt collectors, credit references and utility companies. These issues are discussed in this chapter.

PRICE

The main reason that people buy repossessed properties is the price. In most cases, properties in possession will need to be disposed of quickly and this means that many will be offered at a price that may be more favourable than other properties of similar type that are being sold by owner-occupiers. Although lenders should obtain the best possible price for the borrower who has been evicted, in practice, they tend to try to dispose of the property quickly and are willing to accept offers that may be under the asking, or guide, price. This means that, as a prospective house purchaser, there are bargains to be had, if you know where to look and build up a good relationship with local estate agents. More information about how to do this is provided in Chapters 5 and 8.

Possible savings

According to my research, it is possible to obtain a property at around ten to 15 per cent below the market price. But you should note that this will not always be the case, especially if a bidding war begins on the property in which you are interested (see Chapter 8). Often, the greater the bargain, the poorer state of repair the property has been left in, so you may need to undertake considerable improvement and development of the property to make it habitable and suitable for your needs. Also, you may find that you are competing with experienced property developers and investors for this type of bargain, so you need to understand how to beat the competition. More information about how to do this is provided in Chapter 5.

 *'When we saw how much it was on sale for, we thought that there must be something wrong with it. But we went to have a*

look and it was lovely. So lovely and so cheap. We couldn't believe it. It was by far the cheapest one in that part of Bournemouth, because, you know, house prices had gone up so much around there. Some of them we just couldn't afford. But this one we could. I can't really tell you when we found out that it had been repossessed. I just can't remember. But that explained it to us why it was so cheap.'

Sandra, Bournemouth.

 AUTHOR'S NOTE

Recent media reports have suggested that some property investors are now able to buy properties that are up to 70 per cent cheaper than their market value because they have been repossessed and are in such a poor state of repair. I must point out that our firm has never been able to do this and I have not come across anyone in my research who has achieved such an exceptional bargain. If I were an evicted owner, I would certainly consider taking the lender to court if it sold my property so cheaply.

Buyer beware

You should note, however, that if the property has been sold at too low a price or if house prices are rising rapidly in the area, it is possible for the previous owner to stop the sale before you exchange contracts by obtaining an 'order for sale' (see Chapters 2 and 3). This can be costly, stressful and time-consuming for you and your family. Therefore, it is important to try to balance your need for a cheap property with the evictee's need to recoup his debt. In some cases, it may be preferable to offer a realistic price that is slightly below the market value, rather than a very low offer that may be accepted by the lender, but contested by the evictee.

Also, some estate agents will decide to advertise your offer in the local paper, or on the internet, with further bids invited that are higher than your offer. This is because they should try to obtain the best possible price for the property. If you have made a very low offer, this could encourage others to offer more, so you need to weigh up the pros and cons of making a low offer. However, there is no legal obligation for an estate agent to advertise your offer and if you can convince him that you are a serious buyer and that you can move quickly on the sale, he may agree not to advertise your offer. Property developers often convince estate agents not to advertise their offer because they can move quickly on the sale (see Chapter 8).

'I just didn't know that they would put my offer in the paper and ask for people to offer more. I just didn't know that…And of course people did offer more and we lost the house. It's hard, isn't it? Next time do I offer more so I don't lose the house? It was in the housing section of the paper so I think loads of people saw it…The advert was really quite big. I don't know; it's a difficult one.'

Alex, Portsmouth.

SPEED OF SALE

Most lenders wish to sell properties in possession as quickly as possible so that they can recover the debt owed to them. Also, because the previous owners have been evicted, or have abandoned or surrendered their property, the property is not part of a chain and a quick sale can be realised. This is of particular appeal to property developers and investors who are hoping to make a quick turnaround on the property, either to let to tenants or to sell on at a profit:

'As a property developer I don't want to be tied up in long chains…often they break down and I don't want to waste money when this happens. It's taken me a long time but my contacts trust me now and they'll let me know as soon as something comes to them, you know, a repossession bargain. Sometimes it's really quick and that's what I need. Time is money.'

Mark, Southampton.

But not all properties that have been repossessed move quickly, so it is important to discuss how long a property has been on the market with the estate agent or auctioneer. There may be scope to offer a lower price if a property has been on the market for some time.

Moving quickly

You should note that you will increase your chances of obtaining a bargain property if you are able to move quickly on the sale. You can do this if you are not part of a chain and if you have your mortgage arrangement in place or you are a cash buyer. Remember this when you advertise your own property for sale. Consider buyers who offer the best chance of realising a sale, such as cash buyers, first-time buyers who already have a mortgage in place, or property investors. These people may not necessarily offer the best price for your property, but they will not be part of a chain and they will be able to move quickly, thus increasing your chances of your obtaining the repossessed property that you are interested in.

You should note also that some lenders will put you under pressure to exchange very quickly, with some even asking that there is a simultaneous exchange and completion date (see Chapter 10). Exchange of contracts is when the transfer of title/ownership of a property happens. At this time the buyer signs the contract for sale and sends it to the seller, who also signs the document. Both parties are legally bound to complete the transfer once the exchange has taken place and they cannot pull out of the deal. Completion is the last stage of the purchasing process and is the date by which all funds are paid and all documentation is finalised. The house becomes the property of the purchaser on this date.

'I had a case recently where draft contracts were issued on 25 March, received 26 March and their return was demanded within two weeks as an exchange of contracts had not taken place. This is the pressure the buyer will be put under to exchange.'

A P Malam Property Lawyers, Conwy.

ETHICAL AND MORAL IMPLICATIONS

The fact that you are buying a home from which a person or family has been evicted, or departed voluntarily, has to be a matter of personal conscience. When a house is repossessed, the borrower may have several courses of action available to him, including moving in with family and friends, renting privately from a landlord, applying for council or housing association housing, buying another property or becoming homeless.

If he decides to buy another property, he may have difficulty raising a mortgage because he has to tell his new lender that his previous property was repossessed. If a mortgage is refused, he has to tell any other companies to which he applies that this is the case. Some specialist lenders may be willing to provide a loan, but the borrower may have to pay a larger deposit and higher interest rates. Also, if the borrower still has previous debts, the previous lender may be able to put a charge on his new home, which means that, when he comes to sell the new home, the previous mortgage lender may claim part of the proceeds.

Dealing with ethical issues

Buyers of repossessed property deal with ethical issues in different ways. Some believe it is nothing to do with them, while others think that they have helped to alleviate the problems of the person who has lost their home:

'Really, I think it's their own fault. I wouldn't get into that situation myself because I'm sensible and know how to run my finances. It's a mug's game borrowing too much. OK, I've got a mortgage, but I'd never stretch myself like that and I'd always make sure I'd got the right type of insurance. So, no, I don't feel guilty about it really, not at all.'

Colin, Bristol.

'Yes, I did worry about it quite a lot actually. But then Peter said, well, you know, if we hadn't bought the house, they would still be in trouble...so really I think we've probably helped

them out. Obviously I don't know what debt they had, but at least they've sold their house and I presume they've paid off their debts, so, yes, I think we helped them out actually.'

Joan, Northampton.

Personal items

Another ethical dilemma was raised, during the research for this book, by a property developer who pointed out that one of the hardest things about buying repossessed property was that people vacate the property very quickly, often leaving personal items behind. Some leave at the last minute, without having had time to pack all their belongings. In one of the repossessions he had bought, he found some very personal items, such as wedding photos, pictures of the children, christening gowns and children's certificates and badges. He approached the estate agent to ask where he could send these items as he felt it was wrong to put them in a skip because they were so personal, but neither the estate agent nor the lender would tell him the new address, and they would not agree to forward the items themselves. Eventually, the property developer had to throw the items away, which upset him.

He pointed out that this happened quite often with repossessed properties because some evictees leave very quickly, especially if they are abandoning the property without informing the lender, and they often forget about, or cannot take with them, items stored in lofts or basements. He said that this can be 'hard to cope with sometimes' and that he often 'felt very guilty' when he had to throw away personal items.

Disposing of personal items

If you buy a repossessed property, you need to realise that this situation could arise and you need to be prepared to deal with the issue in the best way that you can. Often lenders and estate agents do not know the whereabouts of previous occupants and they cannot pass on confidential information to you. Also, they have no obligation to pass on belongings or personal items once a person has been evicted from their property, if the correct procedures have been followed. If belongings have not been removed, the lender is entitled to dispose of them, prior to the sale of the property. But most lenders will not enter lofts and basements, so this job may fall to you and your family, once you have purchased the property.

AUTHOR'S NOTE

Our firm once found a couple of vases in the loft of a property that we had bought. We could not find out who the previous owners were so, after much discussion, we auctioned the vases and gave the money to our local children's hospice. We felt this was the best way to deal with the dilemma, even though it meant that the previous family were unable to recover what could have been family heirlooms.

You should note, however, that some purchasers do not encounter any of these ethical and moral dilemmas when they are purchasing a repossessed property, even though they might have expected to, as Sandra points out in the quotation below:

'I'd thought I wouldn't be able to do it, you know, buy a house which had been repossessed. But it was too good to miss, so I put an offer in and it was accepted. Actually, it was no problem at all. I still felt bad, but when we didn't have any trouble with bailiffs or anything I felt better. We found out that the person had split up from his wife. So they couldn't pay the mortgage and he left because he didn't want the house anyway. So although I felt a bit bad, I didn't in the end. The house was lovely and we had no problems at all.'

Sandra, Bournemouth.

DAMAGE AND STRIPPED FIXTURES AND FITTINGS

As we have seen previously, repossessed properties can be left in all sorts of conditions. Some properties are left in very good condition and new owners do not encounter any problems with damage when they move in. But some people, when they know that their property is going to be repossessed, will strip it of all fixtures and fittings, whereas others may cause damage through anger and/or upset. Detailed information about the type of problems that can be caused is provided in Case Study 6, Chapter 11.

Often, when you are viewing a property, this type of damage is the first indication that the property has been repossessed. Although statistical research has not been conducted into the issue, anecdotal evidence from estate agents and lenders seems to suggest that properties that have been abandoned tend to have more damage and stripped fittings, perhaps because borrowers take time to plan their departure before lenders realise that there is a problem (see Chapter 2).

Type of damage

The type of damage varies considerably. Some properties are so badly damaged and stripped that they can only be offered at auction to investors and developers who are willing to spend money on making the property habitable again. If you are interested in this type of development project, you may be able to obtain a good bargain at the auction, but you will have to be prepared to put in the work required, or spend enough money employing others, to make the property habitable. You may have to budget for a new kitchen, new bathroom, new central heating system, including radiators and boiler, light fittings and flooring. You will also have to make sure that the property is in a safe condition by obtaining a full structural survey and gas and electricity safety checks. More information about doing this is provided in Chapter 7. This is because electrical and gas appliances can be taken from properties without first being safely disconnected and, in other cases, previous owners have deliberately sabotaged the property, leaving it in a dangerous condition.

'There was a lot of damage – floors had been stamped through, ceiling tiles knocked down, bolts from the loft ladder removed, broken glass put down plug holes and drains. And the worst thing was that some of this damage happened after we'd made an offer. Nobody really knows how, but at the moment we're fighting with the estate agent to get some money for the damage.'

Stuart, Northampton.

AUTHOR'S NOTE

It is possible for Stuart to ask for compensation in the form of a reduction on the selling price of the property, but any redress for damage should always be agreed before the exchange of contracts takes place and some lenders may be reluctant to offer a reduction for fear of being sued and/or because the selling price will not cover the loan. Ultimately, the cost of any damage caused by previous occupants will be borne by the evicted owners themselves, because the property will be sold for less, yet they still have to repay the whole loan, or the lender will make the necessary repairs and add the cost to the debt owed by the evicted borrower.

It is unlikely that a lender would decide to make a claim against an evictee for damages or, indeed, whether it would be worth its while doing so. This is because the lender is able to chase the full amount of the loan from the borrower, regardless of whether the property sells for the full amount (see Chapter 3). It is also possible for a lender to take out insurance on the loan which will cover 'in possession risks'. This could include cases of damage or where it is unable to obtain vacant possession on a property that it has repossessed because a squatter has taken unlawful possession, for example.

PROBLEMS WITH DEBT COLLECTORS

If you choose to buy a repossessed property, you may encounter problems with creditors and debt collectors who are looking for the previous owners. This can occur by telephone, if you have kept the same telephone number, or, more commonly, by post and personal visits. Some debt collectors have contacted neighbours, asking if they know who owns the property or the whereabouts of the previous owners:

'Oh yes, we've had quite a few problems. Why are debt collectors big bald-headed men…well, I suppose that's obvious if they want to get the job done. And really I guess they were OK when we told them it was nothing to do with us. But we got letters and visits and letters to the neighbours, what, for

about six months, I would say, and then it all died down. It's a bit cheeky, isn't it, sending letters to the neighbours? Luckily, they [the neighbours] came and told us. I get the impression people didn't much like the family who used to live here. So the neighbours have been good really, haven't they?'

Mrs Adams, Gloucestershire.

Alleviating the problems

Although problems with bailiffs and debt collectors can be annoying and take up your time, there are a number of things that you can do to try to reduce or alleviate the problems, such as informing the relevant organisations that you have bought the property and insisting that written records held by credit agencies are updated. More information about doing this is provided in Chapters 11 and 12.

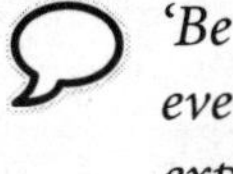

'Be prepared for a lot of post from debt collectors or maybe even visits from bailiffs. I decided to print lots of labels which explained that the post was being returned as the house had been sold by the bank through the estate agent, and I made sure I specified which ones, with contact numbers on the labels. I also put the date I completed on the house and that I had no connection with the previous occupier. I would say that I've used about 45 of these labels so far, but I think the post is gradually getting less now. We only get a couple of demands a month now.'

Email from a purchaser who wishes to remain anonymous, south of England.

CREDIT REFERENCE AGENCIES

As a new purchaser, you may initially encounter problems when you try to obtain credit. This is due to the status of the repossessed property. Once a property has been taken into possession, details are passed to a credit

This is an organisation that has been set up to collect and ...ation on a person's financial position in order to provide ...al information to financial organisations, when requested, although it does not express an opinion about the creditworthiness of an applicant. The information held by credit reference agencies can include the following:

- The electoral register.

- Details of County Court Judgments (CCJs) (which are called 'decrees' in Scotland).

- Bankruptcy information.

- Details of Individual Voluntary Arrangements (IVAs).

- Repossession information.

- Credit account information.

- Names and addresses of people who have moved without informing the lender.

- Records of which lenders have made a credit reference check.

- Information about people with the same surname who live with the client.

In most cases, information is held for six years. There are three main credit reference agencies in the UK and contact details of each are provided in Appendix 2: Useful Organisations.

Although your credit rating should not be based on the property, if you apply for credit before the records have been changed on your new property, you may experience problems obtaining credit. This is because the lender uses the electoral register, held by the credit reference agency, to confirm that you live at the address that you have specified. If your name does not appear on the register at that property, you may be refused credit. To rectify this situation, you need to contact your local authority as soon as you move into the property as it updates the electoral register regularly and it sends these updates to credit reference agencies. For information about changing your information that is held by credit reference agencies, see Chapter 12.

PROBLEMS WITH UTILITY COMPANIES

If a previous owner has found himself struggling financially, he may have experienced problems with the utility companies. When a homeowner gets into arrears on his utility supplies, he tends to be given the following options to sort out his problems:

- Make a short-term arrangement to pay the arrears in instalments before the next bill arrives.

- Arrange a payment plan, which includes current usage and arrears, usually over a set period of time.

- Have a prepayment meter installed. This is often used as an alternative to disconnection and you may find that the repossessed property in which you are interested has one installed.

- Be disconnected. This tends to be used as a last resort when all other methods have failed.

Notifying the supplier

When you move into your new home, you must notify the supplier of the date that you moved in and supply a meter reading for that day. This should help to protect you if the utility company tries to charge you for fuel that you have not used. If you wish to change supplier, you must give at least 28 days' notice. In houses where a prepayment meter has been installed, you must transfer the supply into your name – if you use the previous occupant's card or key, any money you pay will be credited to his account. If you have a good previous record with your utility supply company, you can contact the company to find out about changing the prepayment meter.

Although you should not have any difficulty changing your supply, some companies may be reluctant to take you on as a new customer if it notices that there have been previous problems with the property. You should keep details of your last supplier, including your previous address and payment history, so that you can prove that you have not had any difficulty paying bills in the past. But if this does not rectify the situation, and if you continue to have problems with utility supplies in your new home, you should contact Energywatch, which will be able to offer advice about sorting out the problem (www.energywatch.org.uk).

 *'I'd heard stories that people had experienced problems changing electricity supplier, but I must admit that we had no trouble at all. We just informed them when we moved in and then we changed supplier about six months later, when we found one that was cheaper by using one of those comparison websites. As I said before, we were worried that we might have problems, what with it being a repossession, but we had no problems at all. It was great and we've finally been able to afford somewhere in Bournemouth.'*

Sandra, Bournemouth.

SUMMARY

- One of the main advantages to buying a property that has been repossessed is that there is the potential to obtain a property at a bargain price. In some cases, it may be possible to obtain a property at ten to 15 per cent below market value, although, as an ordinary buyer, you may have to compete against property developers and investors to try to gain this type of bargain.

- Another advantage is that the buying process can move much quicker as the lender wants to make a quick sale and there is no chain involved with the property that has been repossessed.

- But there are disadvantages that can become apparent when you are buying this type of property. This includes damage, stripped fittings and fixtures, problems with debt collectors, problems with obtaining credit and disconnected utility supplies.

- Most of these problems are easily overcome with raised awareness, foresight and careful organisation. Also, some people who have bought a repossessed property do not experience any problems at all. If you are still interested in purchasing a repossessed property, once you have weighed up the advantages and disadvantages, you can start to think more about how you are going to obtain details about this type of property. These issues are discussed in the following chapter.

CHAPTER 5:

WHERE DO YOU FIND REPOSSESSED PROPERTY?

'When people first come into the office asking for property details we won't tell them that a property has been repossessed. Usually this is because we're asked not to by the lender. However, we will advertise the fact that an offer has been made on a property and we will ask for further bids. We put this advert in the local newspaper, but, even then, we won't specifically mention that the property is a repossession because the lender still asks us not to, although buyers could make an educated guess that this is the case. It's only when someone makes an offer or seems very keen that we will tell them more about the history of the property.'

Estate agent, Weymouth.

The quotation above illustrates that many estate agents are reluctant to advertise that a property has been repossessed. As we have seen previously, this tends to be because estate agents believe that potential buyers will make a lower offer if they know that the property is a repossession, and that others are unwilling to buy a property that has been repossessed because they believe it will be left in a poor state of repair.

However, as the quotation hints at, it is possible to find out about properties that have been repossessed, even if estate agents are unwilling to pass on this information. This involves gaining an understanding of the marketing and advertising procedures that can be adopted by estate agents and auctioneers, finding out how to register an interest, understanding how to gain a competitive edge and knowing how to spot property that has been repossessed. These issues are discussed in this chapter.

> *'There may be a view that knowing it is a repossessed property will deflate the price. Lenders do not have to advertise that a property has been repossessed. If it is not evident on viewing the property, then it will become evident through the legal process.'*
>
> **The Council of Mortgage Lenders (CML).**

INFORMATION FROM ESTATE AGENTS

In general, it tends to be the larger estate agents or those that are connected to a bank, building society or mortgage company that are asked to dispose of repossessions. Independent or small estate agents are less likely to sell this type of property, although you should approach all estate agents in the area as there are exceptions to this rule.

Estate agents prefer not to use the term 'repossessed' when they advertise property, but if they are pushed about the history of a property, some may talk about 'properties in distress' or 'distress sales'. These euphemisms include properties that have been repossessed and, for example, properties that are being sold when a person has died – both of which have the potential to be offered at a rate below the usual market price or at a price upon which you can negotiate.

This is a block of flats located on the south coast of England. The block was completed in 2004, with several of the flats being sold to people hoping to let them to holidaymakers on weekly or fortnightly lets. But a local estate agent believes that 'at least two' of the flats have been repossessed, although he was unwilling to be more specific about the details. When he was pushed for more information, he said that one flat had been sold recently (June 2008) for £8,200 less than the price of an identical flat sold a month earlier. Although he wouldn't specifically say that this was the case, I took this to mean that a repossessed flat had sold much more cheaply than one that had not been repossessed, thus representing a considerable bargain for the lucky buyer.

When you are using estate agents check to see whether they are a member of the National Association of Estate Agents (NAEA) or the Ombudsman for Estate Agents (OEA), as both organisations have strict codes of professional conduct and they will help you to sort out any problems or complaints that you may encounter (their contact details are provided in Appendix 2: Useful Organisations). More information about buying repossessed property through estate agents and the selling procedures that they adopt is provided in Chapter 8.

Commercially sensitive information

During the research for this book I sent an email to 200 estate agents throughout the UK to find out how many repossessions they deal with in their offices and the procedures that they adopt when they dispose of this type of property. I received the grand total of eight replies. Seven told me that they do not deal with repossessions and another gave the following reply:

'Dr. Dawson

Your email has been passed to me in light of the questions you have raised.

Unfortunately, we are unable to answer any of your questions as they pertain to what would be deemed 'commercially sensitive' material. As a company listed on the London Stock Exchange (LSE), we are bound by its regulations with regard to what business information we make public and how.

On an industry-wide basis, you may find that what you need is available from the Council of Mortgage Lenders (CML). It collates information supplied by all mortgage providers in the UK and it speaks on behalf of the industry. It will also be able to advise you on industry best practice on repossession cases. I attach its details below.

I am sorry that we cannot be of any further help, but we trust that the CML will be of assistance in your enquiries.'

Obviously, some people may not respond to emails of this nature and some email addresses may have been inactive. People can choose not to answer questions for a number of reasons, but I have been a researcher for over 20 years and have never received such a low response rate. To me, this illustrates that the topic of repossessions is an incredibly sensitive issue for estate agents and lenders.

Local estate agents

As the email approach was so unsuccessful, I decided to visit seven local estate agents, posing as a buyer interested in repossessions. Three of them said that they do not, or 'very rarely', deal with repossessions and instead directed me to the larger estate agents in the area. Two said that they sometimes dealt with repossessions, but that they were not able to tell me when this was the case, nor would they advertise the fact that a property has been repossessed. One estate agent said that he was not able to tell me, but he then showed me details of two properties on which the seller was willing to 'negotiate'. I took these to be distress sales on which the seller, whether an individual or a lender, wanted to make a quick sale. The final estate agent said that he did deal with repossessions and showed me details of the only repossessed property that he had on the books at that time, illustrating that some estate agents will provide this information, when asked. This property was 'in need of modernisation' – it did not have a kitchen and it would need a new back door.

 **AUTHOR'S NOTE**

It may sound obvious, but I found that a direct question such as 'Do you sell properties that have been repossessed?' saves a lot of time and effort. There are many estate agents that do not deal with this type of property, so once you know this, you can concentrate instead on those that do sell repossessions. Some will say 'We do, but I cannot tell you

about them'. If this is the case, at least you know to persevere with that agent, perhaps trying a different member of staff on a different day.

INFORMATION FROM AUCTIONEERS

Many repossessed properties are sold at auction. As we have seen previously, this can be because the properties have been left in a poor state of repair and would appeal more to property developers or investors, or because a local auctioneer specialises in selling that type of property. In other cases, properties are sold at auction because a lender has been unable to dispose of it through its preferred channel.

Some of the larger estate agents work closely with auctioneers and will provide information about contacting local auctioneers and/or put you on their mailing list. Some may also provide a booklet and DVD that explains the process of buying property at auction.

If you are interested in buying a repossession at auction, the buying and selling process is quite different, as you have to make sure that you have the cash available upfront and all surveys and checks must be carried out before the auction takes place (see Chapter 9). But if you are willing to buy at auction, there is the potential to obtain a greater bargain than you may do otherwise. The reason for this is that once you have made your bid and it has been accepted, no one else can make a higher bid because you have effectively exchanged contracts on the property. If you choose this option, you have to make sure that you do not get carried away with your bidding and you hope that a bidding war does not occur on the property in which you are interested. If this occurs, you may not be successful in obtaining the bargain you desire.

Finding out about auctions

To find out about local auctions, visit your local estate agents and ask them whether they know of any local auctions in the area. Some will provide you with details of auction houses and you should contact them direct to include your name on their mailing list. They will then send you their catalogues for auctions that are to take place in your area. It is possible to find out about auctions in your area from the internet, but most sites will require you to register and pay a fee, whereas information from estate agents is free for potential purchasers. Contact details of all the principal property auctioneers in the UK are provided in Howard R Gooddie's book 'Buying Bargains at Property Auctions' (which is available from www.law pack.co.uk).

Finding out whether a property is a repossession

In most cases, the term 'by order of mortgagee' is used to describe the sale of a repossessed property at auction, and this term may be used in the auction catalogue and when the property is described during the auction before bidding commences. Other terms that may be used are described in the quotation below. But some auction houses may not advertise a property in their catalogue as repossessed, on instruction of the lender, although they may have advertised the property in the local press and stated that it will be up for auction on a specific date, which can provide a clue that it is a repossession. Also, you will be able to find out more about the property and ask detailed questions during the viewing and, if you take notice of the tips offered below, you will find it easier to spot repossessions that are to be auctioned.

'Some banks and building societies are very coy about the public knowing that they have repossessed properties and take considerable steps to avoid it being known that properties included in auctions are the result of repossessions. Other societies and banks are quite open. You can look for the clues.

In the initial advertisements, the auctioneers may disclose that certain properties are being sold as a result of repossession. The advert may contain a general list of the clients for whom they are selling, which will then include the names of the societies and the banks. This information may be repeated in the auction catalogue itself, either in a general statement or on the relevant lots. The catalogue may give less specific references with phrases such as 'On behalf of mortgagees in possession', 'By order of…Building Society', 'On the instruction of an LPA Receiver' or 'On the instructions of a liquidator' or similar.

Without these clues, there can be more subtle indications. The solicitor acting may have as his address the head office of a building society or bank. Even without that direct indication, it is possible that the name of the building from which the solicitor operates is an indication of the society for which he works. It may even be possible to link up the solicitor's telephone number quoted or the one quoted for access to the property.

If all else fails, an outright enquiry at the auctioneer's office or at the co-agents' office may tell you if the lot you are considering is as a result of a repossession.'

'Buying Bargains at Property Auctions', Howard R Gooddie. (This book is available from www.lawpack.co.uk.)

INFORMATION IN LOCAL NEWSPAPERS

As we have seen previously, lenders are under a duty to make sure that they receive the best possible price for a repossessed property. Therefore, if a selling agent has received an offer on a property, he will advertise it for a period of seven days (or more if there is a lot of interest in the property). This procedure is called the 'notice of offer'. Selling agents use the local press to do this and adverts will appear in the housing or small advertisement section of the newspaper. An example of this type of advert is provided in Chapter 8, and examples of the online version of this 'notice of offer' are provided below.

The advert will provide details of the property and information about the offer that has been made. Further offers are invited, using a 'sealed bid' approach, or asked for in writing. Many of these adverts ask that higher bids are made 'before exchange of contracts', which means that, as a potential purchaser, there is the possibility that someone could offer a higher bid than yours and you could lose the property at any time before you exchange contracts. Also, you should note that my research has uncovered a number of questionable practices with this type of advertising and bidding process, and it is important that you brace yourself for possible disappointment. These questionable practices are described in detail in Chapter 8.

You can increase your chances of finding out about repossessed property by finding out when local newspapers provide information about houses for sale and by reading all of the small advertisements carefully. Often, this can be the first time that you may get an indication that a property has been repossessed; even if the advert does not mention that this is the case.

'I saw a tiny, weeny advert in our evening paper. That's how I found out about it. I needed my glasses though. It said that we could make a higher offer if we wanted. I offered more and, to cut a long story short, I got the place.

'We paid £279,999 in 2007. Unfortunately, I think prices have fallen a bit now, but, at the time, we thought we had done really well. Well, I still think we've done very well. My husband thinks that it was about £5,000 cheaper than it should have been.'

Mrs Adams, Gloucestershire.

USING ONLINE SOURCES

It is possible to find out about repossessed properties online, but be wary of some of the websites that offer to find repossessed property for you as they will charge a fee or commission, which can be quite hefty. If you do decide to use online sources, always check the 'about us' section to find out more about the organisation. Find out what fee is payable and ask whether your registration details are passed on to other companies. Never pay money or pass your bank details to organisations that you do not know enough about or trust completely.

Registering your details online

You can register your details with legitimate estate agents (i.e. members of the NAEA or OEA) and auctioneers online and they will send you information about properties as soon as they come on the market, or send you the latest auction catalogue. Again, they are unlikely to tell you that the property is a repossession, but you will be able to obtain clues about whether this is the case by following the advice offered below. Try to build up a trusting relationship and you may find that you receive more information about repossessed property, once an estate agent realises that you are a serious buyer. Some useful websites that you can try are listed below. Also, if you register with property websites, you may find it useful to open a separate email account as you can be inundated with responses.

Online newspapers

If your local newspaper publishes an online version, you can view past and current 'notices of offer' adverts that appear in the paper. Some of these will indicate that a property is a repossession by using the terms 'by order of the mortgagees in possession' or 'we are acting for the mortgagees'. Others will prefer not to indicate that the property is a repossession (see example online advertisements below). Using online sources such as these is useful to find out how the procedure works in your local paper and to see which houses have been advertised in the past and for how much. As many of these adverts state that higher offers can be made any time before the exchange of contracts, it may be possible for you to find suitable properties on which you can still make an offer.

EXAMPLES OF ONLINE 'NOTICE OF OFFER' ADVERTISEMENTS

Example 1

Location: Liverpool

Price: £ 90,000

NOTICE OF OFFER [*address*]. By order of the mortgagees in possession, we would advise that an offer has been made for the above property in the sum of £90,000. Any person wishing to increase on this offer should notify the agents of his best offer prior to the exchange of contracts. Selling Agent [*address*].

Example 2

[*Address*]. We are acting for the mortgagees and have received an offer of £166,000 on the above property. Any interested parties must submit any higher offers in writing to the selling agent before exchange of contracts takes place. Selling Agent [*address*].

Example 3

The Estate Agent is now in receipt of an offer for the sum of £75,000 for [*address*]. Anyone wishing to place an offer on this property should contact the Selling Agent before exchange of contracts.

REGISTERING AN INTEREST

Although most selling agents are unwilling to let you know when properties have been repossessed, they are very happy to keep you informed of all of the properties that come on the market within your price range. To make sure that this includes repossessed properties, there are certain things that you can point out as desirable when you register an interest with a selling agent:

- Consider the price that you can realistically pay for a property and then add an amount to this figure that you would be able to negotiate off the asking price. This will enable you to obtain details of properties that are out of your price range, but that may be affordable once you have negotiated on the price. The amount that you can add on to the price could be ten to 20 per cent of the asking price. But do not be tempted to ask the selling agent to send you details of properties in all price ranges, or those that are far too expensive, because he will think that you are less serious about making a purchase.

- Point out to the selling agent that you are looking for properties on which you can negotiate, and properties on which the lender wishes to make a 'quick sale'. Point out the advantages you have against other purchasers, which may include the fact that you are a cash buyer, or you already have a mortgage arranged, or that you are not part of a chain. Selling agents tend to spend more time and energy with customers to whom they feel they are more likely to make a sale.

- Point out that you are very interested in obtaining properties that are in need of work and modernisation, and that you will not be put off by properties that have been neglected or badly maintained.

- Try mentioning that you are interested in 'distress sales' or 'properties in distress'. Some selling agents will provide details of this type of property and this will include those that have been repossessed.

- It will help your case if you are flexible about the type and location of the property. All types and sizes of property can be offered as repossessions and if you are very flexible about location and type, you will have the opportunity to find out about a wider variety of properties.

BEATING THE COMPETITION

As a potential purchaser of a repossessed home, you must understand that you are up against savvy property developers and investors who may have built up a good working relationship with selling agents in your area (see Case Study 2 on page 64). To stand a chance of obtaining the bargain you desire, you must understand how to beat the competition. The tips below should help you to do this:

- Get to know your local selling agents. Adopt tricks used by property developers and investors and try to get to know agents and build up a network of contacts. Visit agents on a regular basis and meet the staff, individually. You will find that some members of staff will be more helpful than others, so visit the agents at different times so that you can get to know everyone who works in the office.

- Visit selling agents at times when they are not busy, as they will have more time to talk to you and they will be less distracted. Find out when managers and bosses are present and try to visit at times when they are not available, as some employees are more willing to talk frankly and 'off the record' when their bosses are not listening.

- Obtain a list of all the auctioneers in your area and register on their mailing list so that you can receive catalogues for all forthcoming auctions, as soon as they are published. These catalogues are very useful to your research and will help you to keep abreast of fluctuations in the market and help you to spot bargains when they come up for auction.

- Find out when houses for sale are advertised in your local newspaper. Always read the small advertisements, as the law does not require selling agents to make the advert prominent.

- Register with a number of selling agents online and ask them to email property details as soon as they appear in the market. Often you can receive information about a property before details are published, printed and displayed in windows.

AUTHOR'S NOTE

During the research for my book I have been surprised at the number of people who say that they 'do not trust estate agents'. Indeed, my research has shown that many people suspect the agents of acting unlawfully and not in the interests of the buyer. Certainly, over the years that we have run our property company, we have come across some agents who have not behaved in a way that we would expect. When this has happened, we have simply moved to another agent – there are so many estate agents about that you do not have to stick with one that you do not trust. There are many competent and reliable agents about and once we find one, we add them to our list of reliable and trusted contacts.

CASE STUDY 2: ADAM AND DAVID

Adam and David are successful property investors. Their property portfolio is worth a 'significant six-figure sum' and is based in London. Their company has been running for 13 years and they believe that they will be able to cope with recent price drops because they view their investment as a long-term strategy and they are sure that prices will rise again at some time in the future.

The two investors have recently bought three repossessed properties in the same apartment block, which is only four years old. Several of the properties that they already owned were located near to this new development and Adam and David had watched its construction with interest. They thought that it would be useful to buy apartments within the block, but they had been unable to negotiate a good enough price from the developer when the apartments were new.

As property investors for 13 years, they have built up a good rapport with estate agents and mortgage companies in the area. At a meeting to arrange a mortgage on another property, they discussed the new development with the mortgage adviser. He pointed out that they might be better waiting for a few years, that some of the properties were likely to be repossessed because people had paid too much for them and their expectations about the rental income on the properties had been too high.

Sure enough, four years later several apartments appeared on the market in close succession. There were clues to the fact that some of these were repossessions and another meeting with the mortgage adviser confirmed these suspicions. Adam and David approached the estate agent and put in an offer on three of the apartments. No other bids were made during the notification period and the sales went ahead quickly.

Adam put their success down to the fact that they have a very good relationship with their mortgage adviser, who is able to let them know what is happening quickly before other people find out. This relationship has been built over a number of years and they now know the mortgage adviser socially, as well as dealing with him professionally. They are quick to point out, however, that the mortgage adviser only gives them 'general leads' and he does not pass on information that could be considered confidential. (For a list of what estate agents can and cannot do and for advice about making sure that they act ethically and lawfully, see Chapter 8.)

TIPS FOR SPOTTING REPOSSESSIONS

In cases where it is not explicitly mentioned that a property is a repossession, there are clues available. Look out for the following:

- Properties that are offered below the current market value of similar properties in the area. To find out whether this is the case, you will need to monitor the local housing market so that you spot, instantly, when a cheaper property is being advertised. Information about how to do this is provided in Chapter 6.

- Properties on which it is clear that the seller is 'willing to negotiate'. You can find out whether this is the case by asking the estate agent, or noting when a price is advertised with the letters 'ONO' ('or nearest offer').

- Properties with no forward chain. Although this may happen for a variety of reasons, such as death, divorce or moving abroad, if this is combined with any other clues listed here, it may mean that a property has been repossessed.

- Properties that attract 'sealed bids' or 'higher bids', usually over a seven- or 14-day period. This may be advertised by the estate agents in their offices, in the local newspaper and/or online.

- Empty properties. Again, properties may be empty for a variety of reasons, but, if this is combined with some of the clues discussed here, they may be empty due to repossession.

- Tenanted properties on which you are assured vacant possession upon completion, and where there appears to be no private landlord present. This type of property can be offered in other circumstances, but it may be a clue to the fact that it has been repossessed and the lender is letting the property until it is sold. It may be possible to talk to the tenants to find out what is going on.

- Properties that have been stripped of fixtures and fittings. These may be described as 'in need of updating' or 'in need of modernisation' and some estate agents may point out that they will need new doors or windows. Again, this does not necessarily point to a repossession, but it can be a good indication. Also, you may notice that door and window locks have been changed recently, which, again, may be a clue that the property has been repossessed.

 **AUTHOR'S NOTE**

Our firm once viewed a property that we were pretty sure had been repossessed, but, despite constant questioning, the estate agent refused to tell us whether this was the case. The property was tenanted and since we were intending to let the property ourselves, we arranged a meeting with the tenants to find out whether they would be suitable to keep on in the property. They could not tell us whether the property had been repossessed, but pointed out that they were now paying their rent to the mortgage company. In the end, we decided that the property was not right for us, mainly because it was too small, but we were fairly sure that it was a repossession.

SUMMARY

Repossessed property can be offered for sale through estate agents, auctioneers, local newspapers and online sources. It is useful to register an interest with different organisations so that you can obtain information about a variety of properties that are coming on the market. Also, it is important to learn how to recognise clues that a property is a repossession, as most estate agents have been instructed not to pass on this information to potential purchasers. Clues can include empty properties, no forward chain, a price below the market value, a price on which the vendor is willing to negotiate, and properties that have been damaged or are in 'need of modernisation'.

An important part of finding the right property is to undertake a careful and systematic analysis of the property market so that you know what prices are being charged, you know the best locations in which to buy, and you understand how to avoid problem properties. These issues are discussed in the following chapter.

FURTHER READING

Gooddie, H R (2007), *Buying Bargains at Property Auctions*, 4th edition, London: Lawpack Publishing Ltd. (This book is available from www. lawpack.co.uk.)

CHAPTER 6:

RESEARCHING THE MARKET

'There was this house for sale and I thought it was really cheap but my husband didn't think it was cheap…I asked the estate agent all about [it] and he told me that it was a distressed property, or something like that. I can't really remember…My husband said he thought that meant it had been repossessed, but I wasn't sure, you know, I just don't know. The estate agent wouldn't tell us anyway, would he? But what I want to know is how do we know whether it's cheap? The estate agent said it was, but, to be frank, he would say that, wouldn't he? I don't know, it's hard, isn't it?'

Eileen, Weymouth.

In this quotation Eileen makes a very important point, namely, how do you know that a property is being offered at a bargain price? The easiest way to do this is to conduct a thorough price analysis of properties so that you can spot immediately when a bargain property appears on the market. It is a little harder to find out whether the property is a repossession, as Eileen illustrates, but if you follow the advice offered in the previous chapter, this should be an easier task.

There are a variety of sources that you can use to help you to conduct your price analysis, and these are discussed in this chapter. Also, it is important to understand how prices vary in different locations, again, so that you can recognise when a property is advertised below market value for that location. If you are thinking about buying a property in an unfamiliar location, it is important that you thoroughly research the location to make sure that it is suitable for your needs. These issues are discussed in this chapter.

CONDUCTING A PRICE ANALYSIS

When you are conducting a price analysis you should keep abreast of fluctuations in house prices locally and nationally by visiting selling agents, monitoring the local and national press and visiting property websites. If you do this over a period of time, you will get to know the price that is asked for the type of property in which you are interested. This will enable you to recognise when a property is being advertised below market value and this, in addition to the advice offered in the previous chapter, will alert you to the possibility that it has been repossessed.

There are a number of property price surveys conducted each year and these provide a useful way to conduct a house price analysis locally and nationally. These are described below.

The Halifax House Price Index

The Halifax produces the Halifax House Price Index, which was launched in 1984 and is published monthly. On its website you can access the survey data and useful press releases that summarise the data succinctly and coherently (www.hbosplc.com). In May 2008 the Index showed that house prices in the UK fell by 2.4 per cent and that this continues a steady downward trend experienced since the end of 2006.

On the Halifax website you can also access a regional house price map that enables you to click on a region in which you are interested to obtain information about the average house price in the region, the quarterly change and the annual change in prices. This information is compared with the UK as a whole and it provides an efficient way to find out whether a property is being advertised below market value.

A house price calculator is also available on the website. This enables you to enter the price of a property in a selected region to obtain information about how the house price has moved between two specified dates.

Another useful facility is the postcode calculator that enables you to obtain information about average house prices over the years within that postcode area. Again, this is useful to find out whether a property is being advertised below the average house price within that region.

 *'We predict that house prices will be flat during 2008 as a whole. Sound economic fundamentals are supporting house prices. The number of people in employment – a very important driver of housing demand – has risen by 296,000 over the past year to a record 29.40 million. Lower interest rates are also helping to support the economy and the housing market. We predict that the Monetary Policy Committee (MPC) will cut the Bank Rate at least twice more in 2008.'*

Halifax House Price Index, report from February 2008.

The Nationwide

The Nationwide produces a similar survey, based on its mortgage lending. The Nationwide reported that house prices fell by 2.5 per cent in May 2008, which is the seventh consecutive monthly decline. This is slightly different to the information supplied by the Halifax and illustrates that when you are conducting your price analysis, you should use a variety of sources to obtain a clearer picture. Although average prices differ slightly between the two surveys, over the long term their data tends to follow similar patterns because similar research methods are used. But average prices differ between the surveys because the two organisations use slightly different ways of measuring their data (see quotation below).

On the website you can access a useful house price calculator that enables you to enter the price or valuation of a property to find out how the value of the property has changed between specified dates. The Nationwide also produces a number of interesting articles about the property market that can be downloaded from its website (www.nationwide.co.uk).

 *'Nationwide house prices are mix adjusted, i.e. we track a representative house price over time rather than the simple average price. We do not use the simple average price (the Land Registry uses this method) because it is too easily influenced by*

a change in the mix (i.e. the proportion of different property types, locations, etc.) of houses.

Although it remains similar to the Halifax method, we substantially updated our system in 1993, following the publication of the 1991 census data. These improvements mean that our system is more robust to lower sample sizes because it better identifies and tracks our representative house price.'

Nationwide House Price Survey, March 2008.

The Land Registry House Price Index

The Land Registry produces the Land Registry House Price Index, which uses sales data collected on all residential transactions, whether for cash or with a mortgage, in England and Wales since April 2000. It is possible to search the Index at a national, regional, county or London borough level. The survey contains details of over seven million sales and, as it uses such a large sample size, it claims to be the only complete record of residential property transactions in England and Wales.

The Index provides information for each of the nine Government Office Regions (GORs) of England and one of Wales, based on the latest definitions from the Office for National Statistics. (GORs were established in 1994. They 'aim to work in partnership with local people and organisations in order to maximise prosperity and the quality of life within their area'.) At present, these are the areas:

- North East

- North West

- Yorkshire and the Humber

- East Midlands

- West Midlands

- East

- London

- South East

- South West

- Wales

The survey is published on the 20th working day of every month and can be accessed on the Land Registry website (www.landregistry.gov.uk). Again, this produces very useful data for comparing and contrasting house prices in the region in which you are interested.

'The Land Registry has published a quarterly report of simple average prices since 1995. Although the reports are well received and are seen by many as the most comprehensive and authoritative property price data available, we recognise that they do not meet everyone's needs. In particular, these reports lack the statistical sophistication to enable the data to be used as an index of prices. We have tackled this shortcoming by introducing proven statistical techniques from which a monthly measure of the movement of residential house prices in England and Wales can be derived. This initiative is part of a long-standing aim to provide enhanced and more transparent data services for the property market.'

© Crown copyright. 2008 Land Registry.

The Registers of Scotland Executive Agency

If you live in Scotland, a similar survey is produced by the Registers of Scotland Executive Agency (www.ros.gov.uk). By using the online service, you can obtain the selling prices of properties in Scotland. A charge is made for your search (£3.88 in 2008). If you are interested in general figures rather than specific searches, the information is free and it can be obtained from the website. There are also a number of useful press releases and reports that you may find useful for your background research.

The Council of Mortgage Lenders

The Council of Mortgage Lenders (CML) is the trade association for the mortgage lending industry in the UK. It produces regular research articles and in-depth reports on the performance of the housing market. A variety of publications can be downloaded from its website and they are useful for keeping abreast with what is happening in the housing market and for providing advice and information about property investment (www.cml.org.uk). There is a useful mortgage calculator available on the website that enables you to see how much your mortgage would cost on a property in which you are interested.

Home.co.uk

This website provides a comprehensive database of properties in the UK that are advertised for sale on the internet. It also produces information about house prices for buyers, sellers and for people who are thinking about remortgaging their property. The website provides a wide range of useful information to help you when you conduct your price analysis, from enabling you to search house prices by county, city or postcode, to information about setting the correct selling price and knowing when an asking price is right. Again, this information will help you to understand when a property has become available below the current market value.

'The Home.co.uk Asking Price Index is calculated every month using more than 700,000 UK house prices found in the Home.co.uk Property Search Index. This figure represents the majority of the property for sale on the open market in the UK at any given time. Properties above £1 million and below £20,000 are excluded from the calculations.

The Home.co.uk Index is based on asking price data, which means that it can provide insights into price movements around five months ahead of mortgage completion and actual sales data, thus making it the most forward looking of all indices.'

Home.co.uk, March 2008.

CHOOSING A LOCATION

You will increase your chances of obtaining a bargain repossession if you are as flexible as possible about the location in which you wish to buy. Obviously, the price that you can afford has a major influence on the location – once you have conducted a thorough price analysis, you will be able to recognise the average selling price of properties in the area in which you are interested. This will help you to know which areas you can afford to buy in, and which areas are too expensive.

In addition to price, there are other factors that you should take into account when you are choosing a location. The following questions will help you to think more about finding the right location for you:

- Are house prices rising or stable in the area and are they likely to remain so for the foreseeable future? This is of particular importance in this current climate of market uncertainty, where prices are now falling in many parts of the UK. Although you should be able to obtain a repossessed property at below market price, if house prices fall rapidly in the area, you could be left with negative equity on the property and you may struggle to sell the property in the future. Your price analysis should help you to understand how the property market is performing in the area. Also, visit www.propertysnake.co.uk to find out whether house prices are being reduced in that location, and if so, by how much.

- Are there any environmental issues that could have a detrimental influence on the property, your finance or the health of you and your family? This could include the possibility of flooding or problems with pollution. Visit the Environment Agency website and enter the postcode of the property in which you are interested to assess flood potential and to find out about pollution and air quality (www.environment-agency.gov.uk).

- Are there any current or proposed developments or installations that could affect your health or make it harder to sell your property in the future? Visit www.sitefinder.ofcom.org.uk for information about mobile mast sites. View the local authority development plan to find out what development has been proposed for the area.

- Are there any highways planned that could devalue your property? Visit the Highways Agency website to browse road projects by region and for detailed information about each project, whether planned, current or completed (www.highways.gov.uk).

- Would you and your family be happy living in this location? Is there good access to schools, health services, shops and entertainment? Is the area populated with the type of people with whom you and your children could mix, if this is important to you?

- Are there any problems with crime, graffiti and vandalism? Is the area safe?

- If you are buying a property to let to tenants, are there tenants available in the area? Is there room for another buy-to-let landlord in the area or has saturation point been reached? Speak to local letting agents and join your local authority landlord's group as this will help you to network and to find out who else is operating in the area. What rent can you charge, realistically? Will this help you to make a good return on your investment? Was the property let to tenants before it was repossessed? If so, why did the venture fail? Is the failure anything to do with unsuitable location? How can you avoid making the same mistakes?

'We found this lovely place in Gloucestershire. I felt so sorry for the people who'd lost it because it was so lovely. They'd obviously really looked after it. I can't imagine why it was repossessed. Anyway, we looked on that website that shows you a map of the place and how it could flood. The cottage was right in a flood plain and covered in water on the map! Although we really wanted it, we couldn't buy it. It was after the floods of 2007 and we were really worried that it could happen there. It was a shame because it was so lovely.'

Email from a woman living in Cheltenham.

AVOIDING PROBLEM LOCATIONS

There are certain areas that you should avoid, even if you believe you have found the perfect property. This is because you and your family may not be happy living in the property or because you are likely to lose money on your investment and/or find yourself stuck in the negative equity trap. The following list will help you to think about avoiding problem locations:

- **Areas that have been flooded.** You will find it difficult to obtain insurance for your property or you will have to pay a much higher premium. More extreme weather associated with climate change could mean that the area will flood again and there is a possibility that this could become more severe in the future. In extreme circumstances, you could become homeless and lose your possessions.

- **The location of a proposed highway scheme.** The Secretary of State for Transport has the right to buy your land and property, if it is needed for a trunk road scheme, and you must sell the land or property if required, although it is possible to make an appeal. Although you can claim compensation for a road built close to your property, even if you do not have to sell your land, the extra noise and pollution could have a detrimental influence on your quality of life. It will also make it much harder to sell or let your property. These locations should be avoided.

- **An area too close to an airport.** You will find it difficult to sell or let your property and you and your family may become stressed by the noise. For more information about airport expansion and associated problems, visit www.airportwatch.org.uk.

- **Areas of degeneration in which property prices are falling and from which people are moving away.** Empty and boarded up properties attract vandals, squatters and graffiti and they devalue the whole area. Rising crime levels are off-putting for potential purchasers and tenants. Your property could be broken into and, in addition to the upset and worry this causes, your insurance premiums will rise. To find out how an area performs in terms of crime and deprivation, use the postcode search at http://neighbourhood.statistics.gov.uk.

'My parents lived in a place where they had terrible problems with the neighbours. We didn't want to go through all the trouble they'd had, so we made sure we checked everything out first, you know, visited at different times, spoke to some of the neighbours, and all that. I'd probably do it anyway, but we

thought we really had better do it because it was a repossession. Everything was fine. You know, no problems at all. I'm still glad we checked everything out, though, you know, just in case some problems had come up.'

Sandra, Bournemouth.

SPOTTING A BARGAIN

Once you have conducted a thorough price analysis and your comprehensive location research, you should be able to spot when a bargain property appears on the market. The most obvious indication will be that the asking or guide price is below the average market value in the area. Acting quickly will enable you to beat your competitors. To do this successfully, you will need to make sure that you receive information about potential properties from a variety of sources on a regular basis (see Chapter 5).

Savvy property investors also realise the importance of hunting for properties in areas that may not be expensive in themselves, but that are adjacent to areas that are more expensive, or in the process of becoming regenerated. This means that you may be able to acquire cheaper property that rises in value at a quicker rate as the area grows in popularity and becomes regenerated. In terms of property repossessions, you may be able to find a repossessed property that was bought under the Right to Buy scheme on what initially appears to be a run-down council estate, but which has the potential to be regenerated once house prices begin to rise again and more people become owner-occupiers on the estate. Signs that an area is in the process of being regenerated include:

- Empty properties are bought, renovated and refurbished. There are less boarded up properties in the area.

- Derelict land is tidied and developed.

- Householders improve, extend and tidy their properties.

- Small- and large-scale investors and property developers move into the area.

- Fashionable and more expensive retail, food and drink outlets open in the area.

- Neighbourhood Watch schemes, community groups and social activities are set up for local residents.

- Crime rates fall and there are fewer problems with vandalism, burglaries and graffiti.

- Higher earners move into the area, with more expensive cars parked on the driveways.

SUMMARY

If you are interested in buying a repossessed property, you must conduct a thorough price analysis so that you can spot when properties are offered at a price that is cheaper than the average market value. When this is undertaken, along with comprehensive location research, you should be able to spot when bargains are advertised for sale. This will help you to recognise possible repossessions and enable you to act quickly and beat your competitors. If you are flexible about where you can live, you have more scope to obtain the bargain you desire, although you must make sure that the location is suitable and you must recognise and avoid unsuitable locations (e.g. bad areas due to high pollution, high flood risk, unpopular developments or areas of degeneration).

Once you have found a property, you need to assess whether it will be suitable for your needs. This includes viewing the property, researching the neighbourhood and making sure that the property is structurally sound. These issues are discussed in the following chapter.

CHAPTER 7:

CHOOSING A REPOSSESSED PROPERTY

> *'What we found was that they [repossessed properties] weren't coming up very often. So we'd go and see one and then we wouldn't see another one for ages. I'm getting a bit older and forgetful, losing my mind my husband says, but I'd forget what the first one was like when we went to see another. But we didn't want to rush straight in so we never put an offer in, well, for two years anyway. But I did find it difficult to remember. I wish I'd kept records really; then it might have been easier.'*

Ann, Portsmouth.

As Ann points out above, when you go to view a property it is useful to keep records of your viewing so that you can remember the features, especially if you intend to view more than one property. This will also help you to keep a record of the type of properties that are appearing on the market, their condition and the price that is being asked. This is all important background research and it will help you to find the best bargain property in your area.

In addition to this research, you need to know how to get the most out of your viewing, how to ask the right questions to obtain the information you need, how to research the neighbourhood and how to make sure that the house is sound and safe and will not cause you too many problems in the future. This is of particular importance when you are viewing a repossessed property which could have been left in an unsafe condition. These issues are discussed in this chapter.

DEVELOPING A CHECKLIST

When you are choosing a repossessed property, you may find it useful to develop a checklist that will help you to ascertain whether the property will be suitable for your needs. Take your checklist to each viewing as it will provide useful information which you can refer to at a later date and it will help you to narrow down your choices and choose the most appropriate property.

The items that are included on your checklist will depend on your personal wants and needs, and the reasons that you are buying a repossessed property. These should be divided into essential and desirable features, and those about which you are flexible, as illustrated in the sample checklist below. Remember to include the address of the property and the date, day and time that you viewed it.

CHOOSING A REPOSSESSED PROPERTY: SAMPLE CHECKLIST

	Yes	No
Essential		
Below £[price]	___	___
Asking price below market value	___	___
Property prices rising, or stable, in the area	___	___
Good, suitable location	___	___
Three or more bedrooms	___	___
Off-road parking	___	___
Sound structure (no evidence of subsidence, deterioration in the concrete, cracks in the brickwork or bowing roof)	___	___
Located away from a main road	___	___

No obvious development work
on neighbouring land   ____   ____

No restrictions on development in
the title deeds   ____   ____

No obvious boundary disputes   ____   ____

Not located near an airport   ____   ____

Located more than quarter of a mile
from a water course   ____   ____

(This could be a river, stream, ditch, culvert, dyke, sluice or
the sea. Some mortgage companies will not offer a mortgage
on a property that has flood potential and most insurance
companies will require a much higher premium to insure
your property if it is within a quarter of a mile of water.)

No flooding potential   ____   ____

Untenanted   ____   ____

Desirable

Freehold   ____   ____

Enclosed rear garden   ____   ____

Two or more reception rooms   ____   ____

Within two miles of a good school   ____   ____

Within two miles of a GP surgery   ____   ____

New window and door locks   ____   ____

Flexible

Décor (comments after viewing) _______________________

____

____

Facilities in the kitchen (comments after viewing) __________

____

____

Facilities in the bathroom (comments after viewing) _________

____

Type and condition of windows (comments after viewing) _________

____

Condition of doors (comments after viewing) _____________________

____

Condition of fixtures (comments after viewing) __________________

____

Condition of fittings (comments after viewing) __________________

____

Amount and type of insulation (comments after viewing) _________

____

Type and condition of heating (comments after viewing) _________

____

Viewing information

Address ____

____

Date, day and time of first viewing ___________________________

____

Date, day and time of second viewing__________________________

____

Additional comments _______________________________________

____

VIEWING THE PROPERTY

View the property with different senses as this will help you to undertake a thorough examination of the property during your viewing.

Sight

Use your sense of sight to check for problems with the structure of the building. Check that there are no unexplained cracks in the brickwork or that the roof is not bowing (see page 88). As was mentioned in Chapter 1, some local authority housing was made of pre-cast reinforced concrete. If this is the case with the repossession you are viewing, visual signs of serious concrete deterioration are cracks, spalls, rust stains and patches of blown or repaired concrete and if you notice any of these, you should seek advice from a professional. Look for signs of woodworm, rot or decay, and for evidence of subsidence in the brickwork and in the garden. Check that there is a damp proof course in place and make sure that there is nothing around the property that is piled above this level.

'I guess the fact that there was scaffolding on two other houses in the estate should have made us wary, but I didn't think about it. There was a line of red staining down the corners on the front but I didn't even think about that either. It was only when we got a survey done that we found it had concrete cancer. I'd never even heard of that, but the surveyor put the value of the property as well below what they were asking, even though it was a repossessed property. Needless to say, we withdrew our offer.'

House purchaser, Dorchester.

Smell

Use your sense of smell to check for problems with damp, which smells like a cross between urine and fish, or like a rotting mop. Also, check for dry rot – this is a problem that can be expensive to treat and tends to occur in older properties; mainly because kiln dried timbers were not used, roof tiles were generally clay and more porous and most materials did not carry any British Standard specifications. Dry rot has been described as smelling like mushrooms and if you notice this smell, along with a rusty, red dust on wood, floors or carpets, seek further advice from a damp specialist.

Although wet rot may not be quite as dangerous as dry rot, it can still cause significant problems, mainly to external woodwork, but also to internal areas that may get damp, such as bathrooms and kitchens. Use your nose to check for 'musty' smells under cupboards and sinks. If you notice any strong smells, ask the selling agent to explain them and make sure that you receive a satisfactory answer. You may need to seek the advice of an expert if you feel that the problem has not been adequately explained or if you think that the condition is serious.

Sound

Use your hearing to check for noises that could pose a problem, such as heavy traffic, aeroplanes and noisy neighbours. You may find it useful to visit the property at different times of the day and during the evening to find out whether there is a problem with people leaving pubs or nightclubs, or early morning traffic. Also, use your hearing to check for creaky floorboards as these may indicate problems with rot or decay. If there is a central heating system installed, ask the selling agent to demonstrate and listen for any unusual noises from boilers and radiators. If any occur, ask for an explanation.

Touch

Use your sense of touch to feel for bumps, lumps and cracks in the plaster, which could indicate movement or damp, or to feel for crumbling woodwork under the stairs and around windows, which could indicate problems with rot or infestation. Test radiators and hot water to check that they are working efficiently.

Seeing through cosmetic problems

Through undertaking a thorough examination of this type you will be able to gain more of an understanding of the state of the property. It will help you to see through 'cosmetic' problems that may be associated with repossessed property, such as badly maintained décor, and it will enable you to concentrate on the more serious problems that are harder and much more expensive, or extremely difficult, to rectify, such as structural problems. Do not feel uncomfortable about making this kind of thorough inspection, as it is in your best interests to do so. A competent selling agent should enable you to spend as long as you wish on this examination, and if he tries to hurry you along, or avoid your questions, you should find out why.

SPOTTING POTENTIAL PROBLEMS

If you undertake a detailed and systematic viewing of the property, you should be able to spot some of the more obvious problems before you spend money on employing the services of a surveyor. These include the following points:

- Vertical or diagonal cracks in plaster and brickwork, with visible movement of door and window frames, and cracking of concrete paths and areas surrounding the building, suggest subsidence. The most common cause is settlement of the soil, and heavy rainfall and rising water tables can aggravate the problem. Clay soil can shrink over time, which will cause foundations to shift and crack. You should seek expert advice if you notice this type of problem.

- Cracking in brickwork can be caused by nearby tree roots spreading under walls. Also, roots seek out sources of water such as drains, which they can damage. In general, the root system of the tree will be roughly the same size as the bulk of the tree you see above ground, although not all root systems are the same. If there are unexplained cracks in the brickwork, check to see whether trees are causing the problem. Before you cut down a tree, you need to check with your local planning authority that there are no restrictions or that it does not have a Tree Preservation Order (TPO) in place.

- Cracks, spalls and rust stains on concrete can indicate serious deterioration. This is caused by the steel supports within the concrete beginning to rust and react to water and temperature, causing the structure to weaken. Look for these tell-tale signs on load-bearing walls and corners of buildings that have been made of reinforced concrete. Look out for patches of blown concrete, recent repairs or rendering that could conceal the problem. If the outside of the property has been rendered or painted recently, inspect neighbouring properties of similar construction as these may help to provide more clues about the structure of the property. In some cases it is possible to replace the concrete sections of the building, but this is major structural work that can be very expensive, time-consuming and hazardous to undertake. It is highly unlikely that you will be able to obtain a mortgage on this type of property.

- Stains, mould and moisture on external walls can indicate a failing damp proof course or problems with drain pipes and gutters. Check that the ground level has not been raised above the damp proof course and that the vendor has a warranty for the damp proof course if it was carried out recently. This may be included in the Home Information Pack (HIP) (see page 92). Try to view the property when it is raining so that you can check for internal and external leaks.

- Stains, mould and moisture on internal walls and peeling or bubbling wallpaper can indicate problems with damp. Unexplained patches of paintwork that have been touched up recently may be hiding a problem with damp.

- Puddles, mould and cracks in flat roofing may indicate that roofs need replacing and, depending on the size, costs could be significant. View flat roofs from an upstairs window, if possible, and if they look bare or are bulging up in areas, they may be coming to the end of their lifespan. Felt roofs last about ten years, asphalt roofs up to 30 years and good fibreglass roofs will last over 30 years. Ask to see warranties if roofs have been replaced recently. Again, some of these may be included in the HIP.

- Damage to uncovered floorboards or bumps, creaks and bounce in flooring can indicate some type of rot or decay caused by pest infestation. Look for tiny holes and small piles of sawdust, which indicates that the activity is recent and ongoing. Wood-boring beetles thrive in warm damp areas, so look in places where the timber is usually exposed, such as under the stairs or in cupboards.

- Chimneys are susceptible to movement and deterioration of pointing. This can lead to damp patches appearing in ceilings around chimney breasts. Also, check that the chimney is not leaning and looks plumb.

- Recent alterations, such as loft conversions and extensions, should be checked for workmanship and all planning and building controls paperwork should be included in the HIP. If relevant paperwork cannot be produced, you should obtain expert advice about the standard of construction and the building work undertaken. If work has not been carried out in accordance with the regulations, in theory it would be possible for your local authority to apply to a Civil Court for an injunction to have the work undone, although in practice this rarely happens. But you could consider taking out a Building Regulation Indemnity Policy, which is an insurance policy that pays out in the event of enforcement action being taken.

Obtaining expert advice

If you spot any of the problems mentioned above, it is advisable that you obtain a second opinion from an expert, and make sure that this is someone who is independent of the lender or selling agent. If you are buying a property at auction, you will need to make sure that this is done prior to the day of the auction (see Chapter 9 for more information about buying at auction). You should also commission an independent survey of the property (see page 95). Once you have obtained expert advice, ask for a quotation for remedial work and then negotiate for a price reduction. There will be more room to negotiate a lower price if the property has been on the market for a while.

ASKING QUESTIONS

When you are viewing a repossessed property, you should ask a variety of questions of the selling agent. These include the following:

- **Why is the house for sale?** (This is a standard question to ask about any property that is for sale. In some cases the selling agent will admit that it is a repossession, especially if you seem keen on the property during the viewing.)

- **For how long has the property been empty?** (This will help you to know whether you could try offering a lower price than you might otherwise do, if the property has been on the market for some considerable time, and especially if property prices are falling in the area.)

- **For how long has the property been tenanted (if relevant)?** What type of tenancy agreement is in place and how much time is left on the agreement? Will there be vacant possession upon completion?

- **What is the type of ownership on the property?** This could include freehold, leasehold or commonhold. These different types of ownership are described in detail in Chapter 10.

- **Is the property a repossession?** (You can try asking this outright if you have not received a satisfactory answer when you asked why the property is for sale. Some selling agents will let you know that it is a repossession if you ask a direct question during the viewing, once you have established a certain amount of rapport.)

- **Does the selling agent know why the property was repossessed?** (This question is a bit cheeky, and the agent does not have to answer. But you will find that some are willing to discuss this matter in more detail if it looks as if you are interested in the property. This is of particular use to you if you are hoping to let the property and you find that a previous buy-to-let investor was unable to make the investment work.)

- **Has the property been altered in any way and if so, are all the necessary documents included in the HIP (in England and Wales) or the home report (in Scotland, which is available from December 2008 – see page 92)?** This should include planning and building control consents, completion certificates and warranties. If the paperwork cannot be produced, find out how long ago the alteration was completed, who commissioned and undertook the work and whether the lender would be willing to reduce the price for any required indemnity insurance or remedial work. Some of this information may not be readily available, but you should push the selling agent to find out, if you are interested in making an offer.

- **Are there any communal areas within the property and if so, who is responsible for their maintenance?** Is there a service charge payable for repairs and maintenance? How much is this service charge (see Chapter 10)?

- **Does anyone have the right to cross the boundaries of the property? Has there ever been any dispute with the boundaries?** (The selling agent may not know this information, but he should be able to get hold of information about boundaries from whoever holds the deeds to the property, which could be the lender if the property has been repossessed or they could be available from the Land Registry if the property is registered.)

- **What is included in the sale?** Is the lender willing to replace any fixtures and fittings that may have been removed or damaged? If a property has been on the market for some considerable time, the lender may be more willing to negotiate about this issue. But you have to use your discretion on this point as some lenders will undertake the work you require and then add the cost of this work onto the debt owed by the person who has been evicted.

RESEARCHING THE NEIGHBOURHOOD

When you have found a property that appears to be suitable for your needs, you need to conduct your neighbourhood research so that you can find out whether you and your family, or your tenants, would feel comfortable and happy living in that area. Issues that you should be aware of when you are considering a suitable location are discussed in Chapter 6 and you should take note of this advice when you are checking out the neighbourhood. In addition to this advice, you can find out more about whether the neighbourhood is suitable by adopting the following strategies:

- **Speak to the neighbours.** Approach several people in the area, either by knocking on doors or through the local services, such as pubs, shops and churches. Try to find out more about the level of community involvement, such as art classes, babysitting groups, youth centres or reading groups. The type of groups that have been established will give you a good idea about the type of people who live in the neighbourhood and they will help you to understand whether you and your family, or your tenants, would be able to integrate.

- **Visit the area with your whole family, at different times of the day.** Walk through the neighbourhood, as this gives you a different perspective to that obtained by driving. If you have young children, find out about local play areas and visit them with your children. This will help you to check out the facilities and find out who else uses them. Children can be very good at breaking ice and mixing with others, which will help you to decide whether your children would be able to fit in and make friends in the area.

- **Visit local schools, colleges and universities, if they are relevant.** Consult league tables if you wish, but many academics feel that these are not the best indicators of the standard and type of education provided. Instead, talk to teachers and other parents. Get a feel for whether the facilities would be suitable for your child.

- **Visit leisure, entertainment and social facilities in the area to find out whether these would be suitable for your family or your tenants.** You should note that many buy-to-let investments fail because investors have tried to market their property at the type of tenants that would not move into the neighbourhood because leisure, entertainment and social facilities in the area are not what they want or desire. If you are hoping to let your property, you must make sure that your tenants would be happy in the area and that their specific needs would be catered for.

UNDERSTANDING THE HOME INFORMATION PACK

All sellers of homes in England and Wales will need to produce a HIP before they can put their property on the market. In Scotland, a similar system is to be introduced in December 2008 and it will be known as a home report or purchaser's information pack. It is unlikely that the HIP or home report will alert you to the fact that a property has been repossessed if the estate agent or lender does not wish you to know this information. It is not a legal requirement that this information must be included in the pack and most selling agents will choose not to do so for fear of deterring potential buyers.

A HIP in England and Wales contains both compulsory and optional documents, as detailed below.

- **Compulsory:**

    - An index.

    - An Energy Performance Certificate, which shows you how energy efficient the property is on a scale of A to G.

    - A sale statement that includes the address of the property, whether it is freehold, leasehold or commonhold, whether there is vacant possession and information about whether or not the property is registered.

    - Standard searches, such as the local land charges register, planning decisions, road building proposals and the provision of drainage and water services.

    - Evidence of title that proves that the seller owns the property and has the right to sell. It should include a copy of the title plan and an official copy of the individual register for the property, held by the Land Registry. This is made up of the following:

        - a property register, containing a description of the registered land;

        - a proprietorship register, stating the nature of the title, the name and address of the proprietor of the land, and any entries affecting the right of disposal of the land; and

        - a charges register containing charges (such as a mortgage) that affect the land.

- **Optional:**

    - A Home Condition Report (HCR), which contains information about the physical condition of a property (see page 96).

    - A legal summary of the documents, which makes them easier for the buyer to understand.

    - Home use/contents forms, such as information about boundaries, notices, services and planning permissions.

    - Other documents, such as guarantees and warranties, and information about rights of way and ground stability.

Selling agents should provide the pack free of charge if they believe you to be a serious buyer, although they are able to make a reasonable charge for the cost of copying and posting the pack. When you have received a pack, make sure that you check that all the compulsory elements are included and that you understand all of the information. If you are uncertain about anything contained within the pack, seek clarification from the selling agent. More information about HIPs can be obtained from the government's Home Information Pack website (www.homeinformationpacks.gov.uk) or from the Association of Home Information Pack Providers (www.hip association.co.uk).

In Scotland, the home report, or purchaser's information pack, will consist of three documents:

1. A single survey, which gives buyers detailed information about the condition and value of a home before an offer is made.

2. An energy report, which gives a home's energy efficiency rating and its environmental impact in terms of carbon dioxide emissions.

3. A property questionnaire, which contains information, such as a home's Council Tax band, parking facilities, any local authority notices that affect it and alterations that have been made to the home.

More information about the home report or purchaser's information pack in Scotland can be obtained from www.scotland.gov.uk.

Redress schemes

A HIP can be produced by a specialist HIP provider, the vendor or the selling agent. For repossessed property, it will almost certainly be produced by the selling agent. All selling agents in England and Wales marketing a property requiring a HIP must belong to an approved redress scheme. This means that, as the consumer, you have access to redress if you have a complaint about a HIP that has been produced by the selling agent. At present, the following three schemes have been approved by the government for the purpose of dealing with HIP-related complaints:

1. Ombudsman for Estate Agents' HIPs redress scheme (www.oea. co.uk).

2. The Royal Institution of Chartered Surveyors' Surveyor Ombudsman Scheme (www.rics.org).

3. IDRS Ltd Property Adjudication for Consumers Scheme (PACS) (www.idrs.ltd.uk).

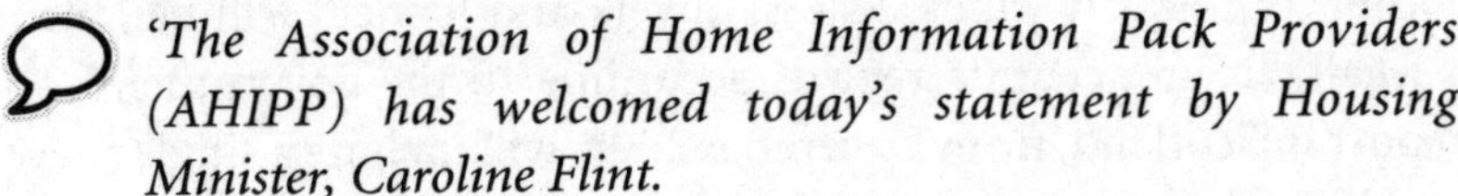

'The Association of Home Information Pack Providers (AHIPP) has welcomed today's statement by Housing Minister, Caroline Flint.

The publication of the results of the government's area trials clearly show that consumers believe the new home buying and selling process is much improved with 72 per cent of consumers being fairly, or very, satisfied with HIPs.

The results evidence a ten per cent reduction in the time taken to reach exchange of contracts, reducing the stress incurred during this period of great uncertainty, and allowing consumers to plan their move with greater confidence. One of the key objectives of HIPs is to speed up the process and clearly this is being achieved.

The seven per cent of consumers that said HIPs have helped them in making the decision whether to buy or not appears low. However, the government figures show that, in many cases, buyers did not see the HIP, so the real figure is far higher, perhaps more like 17 per cent. There is no doubt that this will be a vital factor in reducing transaction failure – one of the other key objectives of the implementation of HIPs.'

**Association of Home Information Pack Providers,
6 March 2008.**

In Scotland, local authority trading standards officers will be responsible for the enforcement of duties associated with the home report or purchaser's information pack.

ARRANGING A SURVEY

You should arrange a survey on a property that you are thinking of buying as this will alert you to any problems and it could save you considerable amounts of money. In some cases, you may find that a Home Condition Report (HCR) has been arranged by the seller on a voluntary basis, and some selling agents who are selling repossessed property will do this to make the purchasing process easier for potential buyers. This will be included in the HIP and should contain 'information about the physical condition of a property, which sellers, buyers and lenders will be able to rely on legally as an accurate report', according to the government. The home report in Scotland, from December 2008, will include a single survey that should be fairly detailed and include information about the condition of the property and urgent repairs or replacements that may be required. But you will need to inspect this report thoroughly and, if you are in doubt about any of the issues raised, you should seek expert advice from a fully qualified surveyor (see below).

 *'The Home Condition Report is an objective report on the condition of a property that can be relied upon by buyers, the seller, lenders and other professionals involved in the conveyancing process.*

The Home Condition Report is produced by a licensed Home Inspector, following an inspection of the property. The report is electronically generated in a standard format to ensure that information is consistent and easy to use and understand.

The Home Condition Report is designed to highlight any defects in the property that are either urgent or serious, in addition to providing a general summary of all other parts of the house. The purpose of the report is to enable the home owner and the ultimate buyer to be aware of defects in the property that may influence decisions in the home buying process.'

The Royal Institution of Chartered Surveyors (RICS), 4 April 2005.

In England and Wales, at this present time, the HCR is a voluntary component of the HIP and if it is not included, you should arrange for your own survey to be undertaken on the property. Indeed, there is some controversy about the quality of these reports, and some experts are advising potential buyers to obtain their own separate, independent survey, even if an HCR has been produced. This should be in addition to the mortgage valuation that is arranged by your mortgage company. Your lender arranges a mortgage valuation because it is concerned with problems that may affect the security of the loan, but this is not a detailed structural report. Mortgage companies charge for this basic valuation, usually in the region of £100–£400, so you will need to pay this cost in addition to the cost of an independent survey, unless the cost is included as part of your mortgage deal.

'We thought that the mortgage valuation would be enough really. I didn't think they'd lend us money if there was a problem. But when my wife stripped the wallpaper in the hall and could see through to next door, we knew we were in trouble!'

Email from a person who wishes to remain anonymous, Southampton.

There are two main types of survey that you can arrange for the property, as detailed below. To obtain contact information of a chartered surveyor in your area, use the Royal Institution of Chartered Surveyors' online database (www.ricsfirms.com).

Homebuyer's report

This type of survey is more comprehensive than the basic valuation that is carried out by your mortgage company. It is most suitable for conventional properties built within the last 150 years, which are in reasonable condition. The survey covers major and minor faults within the property and it should point out the implications of these faults for you, as the potential buyer. The survey will alert you to problems with the structure of the building and damp tests should highlight problem areas in both the interior and exterior of the property.

But while this type of survey assesses the general condition and faults within accessible parts of the property, the surveyor will not lift carpets, move furniture, test wiring or look at parts of the property that are difficult to access. This means that certain conditions could be missed, so, if you are in doubt or the property is older or dilapidated, you should arrange a full structural survey. The homebuyer's report will include the cost of reconstructing the building in the event of damage for insurance purposes. This type of survey will usually cost in the region of £300–£450.

Full structural report

A full structural report, or building survey, is a more comprehensive survey that is suitable for all residential properties and provides information about the construction and condition of a property. It is the most suitable type of survey for older properties, listed buildings, empty and/or dilapidated properties, houses that have been renovated or altered, properties that have been damaged and any other property over which a shadow of doubt may hang, such as those of 'non-traditional construction'.

With this type of survey, all major and minor faults are assessed, along with various tests for damp, condition of timbers, damp proofing, insulation, drainage and other structural conditions. As the surveyor is legally obliged to include all his findings while he is assessing the property, the report is very detailed and can appear quite off-putting. But you should read the report carefully and seek clarification from the surveyor about the conditions that have been uncovered, as some may not be as bad as your initial reading of the report may suggest. In some cases, the surveyor will recommend that specialists are brought in to offer advice about specific conditions. If this is the case, it is advisable that you follow their advice as you will be able to understand more about the condition and the costs involved in putting it right.

'It was when I found a car jack holding up the kitchen floor that I wished I had got a full structural survey done.'

Email from a person who wishes to remain anonymous, Southampton.

Some structural reports may alert you to problems that are too expensive and/or extremely difficult to rectify. In some cases, previous owners, who have struggled financially, may have been tempted to make alterations to their property themselves or use 'cowboys' who have not applied for the relevant permissions and who have undertaken shoddy and dangerous work. Although you will not be able to get back the money you have spent on the survey, it may be prudent in this situation to walk away from the property and find another property with fewer problems. This type of survey will cost in the region of £600–£1,000, depending on the location, type and size of the property.

Structural warranties

If the repossessed property is less than ten years old, it should come with a structural warranty to protect its owner against the risk of latent defects, although this is not a mandatory requirement. Recent media reports, however, have highlighted a number of problems with defects in newer properties, so it is advisable to obtain a separate survey, even if the property has a warranty. This is of particular importance if the repossessed property has been damaged by the previous occupants or if structural defects have been found in neighbouring properties.

OBTAINING SAFETY CHECKS

Some repossessed properties have been left in such a poor state that they are unsafe. Although the lender should make sure that the property is in a safe condition when it is put on the market, my research has shown that this is not always the case. You may find it prudent to obtain your own safety checks, for peace of mind.

If you are intending to let your property, you will be required to ensure that gas fittings and flues are maintained in a safe condition and that an annual safety check is carried out on each gas appliance/flue. Also, you will need to ensure that all electrical equipment is maintained in a safe condition and arrange for either an annual safety check or a new check after each tenancy. If you obtain a safety check before you buy the property, you will gain a better understanding of the work that will be required before you can let your property.

All safety checks and maintenance work must be carried by an installer who is registered with the appropriate government-approved body:

- Electrical installations should be inspected by a professional electrician who is registered with the National Inspection Council for

Electrical Installation Contracting (NICEIC) (www.niceic.org.uk) or the Electrical Contractors' Association (ECA) (www.eca.co.uk).

- Inspections on gas installations in your property should be undertaken by a professional registered with the Council for Registered Gas Installers (CORGI) (www.trustcorgi.com).

- Inspections on oil-fired appliances should be carried out by an installer registered with the Oil Firing Technical Association for the Petroleum Industry (OFTEC) (www.oftec.co.uk).

- Inspections on solid fuel appliances should be carried out by an installer registered with the Heating Equipment Testing and Approval Scheme (HETAS) (www.hetas.co.uk).

To obtain contact details of an inspector and/or installer in your area, see Appendix 2: Useful Organisations. More information about obtaining the relevant safety checks once you have bought a repossessed property is provided in Chapter 11.

CASE STUDY 3: PRAKESH

Prakesh has recently left university with a business degree and has decided that he would like to build up a property portfolio with financial backing from his father. Having driven around an estate situated close to his family home, he obtained details of several estate agents that were advertising properties for sale on the estate. He visited each agent to find out more about the properties. Although he did not own any properties at the time, he introduced himself to estate agents as a 'local landlord and property developer'. Prakesh felt that this made them take him more seriously.

Through 'determined persistence' he was able to ascertain that two of the properties had been repossessed and that one of them had been on the market for 'some considerable time'. He viewed this property and found that it had been completely gutted, but his 'gut instinct' was that it was actually in quite good condition, structurally. Despite this gut instinct, he felt that it was prudent to employ the services of a local surveyor.

Once the full survey was complete, Prakesh discussed the findings with the surveyor and it was recommended that a specialist damp company were called in to check some problems with damp walls in the front room and kitchen. Prakesh obtained a quotation for the work, which was £1,200, to inject a damp proof course and re-plaster the front room.

Satisfied that the property was in reasonable condition, structurally, Prakesh made an offer, which was initially £10,000 below the asking price. The lender refused to accept this offer, so Prakesh waited a week and then offered £8,000 below the asking price. He asked the estate agent to point out to the lender that the offer was below the asking price because of the work that was required to make the property habitable. The lender agreed to the offer and Prakesh obtained a repossessed property at a bargain price.

SUMMARY

Once you have found a repossessed property in which you are interested, you will need to carry out detailed and systematic research into the property and neighbourhood to find out whether it is suitable for your needs. You will find this easier to do if you develop a comprehensive checklist and you understand how to spot potential problems. Also, it is important to arrange a survey so that you can find out whether there are any problems that would be too expensive or difficult to rectify. You should inspect the HIP carefully as this will provide important information, including the results of local searches, an Energy Performance Certificate and information about the type of ownership. But the HIP does not have to point to the fact that the property is a repossession.

There are two main ways that you can buy a repossessed property: through an estate agent or at auction. Buying repossessed property from estate agents is discussed in the following chapter.

FURTHER READING

Ambrose, P (2007), *Home Information Pack Kit*, London: Lawpack Publishing Ltd. (This kit is available from www.lawpack.co.uk.)

CHAPTER 8:

BUYING REPOSSESSED PROPERTY FROM ESTATE AGENTS

'No, I didn't have any problems with the estate agent. She was courteous and efficient. She knew her job really well. We put an offer in and she explained the process to us, which was good because we didn't really know what would happen. My partner has had some trouble with an estate agent in the past, but this one was fine. I can't remember whether she told us that it was a repossession or whether we found out somehow else. I just can't remember. But no, we didn't have any problems at all.'

Sarah, Bournemouth.

During my research for this book I've come across a number of people who have had bad experiences when they are trying to buy a repossessed property through an estate agent. For some, the experience was too disappointing and they decided not to pursue their desire for a repossessed property. But many other people, as illustrated by Sarah above, have successfully bought a repossessed property through estate agents. They have been able to do this because they have been told about the buying and bidding procedure once an offer has been made, they have approached conscientious estate agents who act ethically and lawfully, and they have fought hard for the property they desired. These issues are discussed in this chapter.

MAKING AN OFFER

Once you have found a repossessed property that you are interested in, and you decide to make an offer, make sure that your offer is put to the lender. Some estate agents will tell you that the vendor will not accept an offer below the asking price, but this is often not the case. Obviously, both the lender and estate agent want to receive the best possible price for the property and some may try to do this by telling potential purchasers that the price is non-negotiable. In most cases, this is not true – all lenders will be willing to negotiate if they believe that someone is serious about buying the property.

When you are making an offer, decide on the maximum price that you are willing to pay for the property, and begin by offering well below this price, as illustrated in Case Study 3 (see Chapter 7). Your background research and price analysis will help you to know how much to offer (see Chapter 6). If the vendor wants to make a quick sale, you may have your offer accepted, although the estate agent may then choose to advertise your offer and invite higher bids (see below).

Notice of offer

When estate agents receive an offer on a repossessed property, many will advertise that this offer has been made and invite higher offers. As we have seen previously, this is because the lender is under a 'duty of care' to ensure that it receives the best possible price for the property. But there is no law requiring that estate agents adopt this procedure and, in some cases, you may be able to persuade an agent not to advertise your offer, if you can convince him that you are a very serious buyer and if you can move quickly on the sale.

If an agent does choose to place a notice of offer, advertisements of this nature tend to be placed in the housing, small advertisement or public notice section of the local newspaper. Most advertisements of this type will not mention the fact that the property is a repossession, for fear of putting off potential purchasers. Although the type of advert may vary slightly, the example below provides an illustration of what to expect.

PUBLIC NOTICE

[*The estate agents*] are now in receipt of an offer
for the sum of £175,995 for [*address*].

Anyone wishing to submit an offer on
this property should contact
the estate agents at the address below
before the exchange of contracts.

Some of the advertisements will also contain a picture of the property, especially if the estate agent believes that the property looks desirable and will, therefore, attract further bids. This can be problematic if you have placed a bid on the property, because it may mean that more interest is then shown and a bidding war begins (see Case Study 4 on page 108). This is why it is important for you to set a maximum limit that you can afford to pay for a property and you must make sure that you are not tempted to bid more if a bidding war begins.

UNDERSTANDING THE BIDDING PROCEDURE

Most estate agents will advertise an offer on a property for a period of seven to 14 days. In some cases, the estate agent will invite 'sealed bids', which means that all bids are invited up until a specified date when, in theory, the highest bidder obtains the property. This type of procedure may occur when there is a lot of interest in a property, or it may be the preferred option adopted by the estate agent. In other cases, the estate agent will prefer to use an 'open bid' procedure, where higher bids are invited up until the exchange of contracts. These two procedures are described below.

Sealed bids

During a sealed bid procedure, interested parties are invited to make their bid, in writing, and all bids should be opened at the same time with the property going to the highest bidder. It is expected that people who make bids in this way should be able to complete quickly on the property, usually within 28 days. But, in practice, the process can take longer than this period, and the deadline is usually given in an attempt to stop time-wasters. You will have to decide how much you want to offer as, in theory, you are only able to bid once. Once the property has gone to the highest bidder, the estate agent should remove it from the market.

However, you should note that the sealed bid procedure is not legally binding and my research has found that some estate agents allow disgruntled bidders to make further bids, even after the deadline for sealed bids. Also, they allow the property to remain on the market until the exchange of contracts, which means that someone could still make a higher bid at a later stage. While this is not against the law, it can be seen as an unethical practice and it makes it extremely hard and stressful for you, as a potential purchaser. You can try to reduce the problem by making sure that the estate agent removes the property from the market and by asking him to confirm, in writing, that he will not accept any further bids on the property. If an estate agent refuses to do this, you may find it preferable to move on to another property and deal with an estate agent that does not adopt this practice.

Monitoring the sale

You should note that, as the sealed bidding procedure is not legally binding, in some cases people who have made the highest bid pull out soon after they have been offered the property. Often this is because they realise that their bid is too high, or it can be because they are unable to raise the finance or they are unable to sell their existing property. It is important that you keep in contact with the estate agent to check that the sale is going through. By doing this, you may be able to jump in quickly with another bid if the successful bidder pulls out. The estate agent may be happy to accept your bid as it saves his having to begin the process all over again.

'The mortgagee in possession is required to get the best possible price for a property and this is usually through advertising on the open market. Once an offer has been received, then the company will normally require the selling agent to place a

> *public notice in the local newspaper advertising the offer that he has received and inviting better offers to come forward.*
>
> *There are no fixed procedures for an agent to follow, although one would usually expect there to be a notice as indicated above.'*
>
> **Email from the National Federation of Property Professionals, 3 March 2008, Warwick.**

Open bidding

In cases where an open bidding procedure is adopted, the estate agent invites bids from interested parties, returning to previous bidders and asking whether they are interested in making a further bid if their previous offer has been beaten. Estate agents must inform you when another bid has been made on the property, but they are not obliged to tell you how much the bid is worth. This can mean that prices are pushed up considerably if a bidding war begins (see Case Study 4 on page 108).

In my research, some people have speculated that estate agents have told them that a higher bid has been received, even though they cannot guarantee that this is the case. It is unlawful for estate agents to make phantom bids and if you suspect that this has happened, you should consider making a complaint (see page 113). Reputable estate agents will tell the original bidder that their offer has been beaten and invite further offers based on this information.

Keeping in contact

If there are several people making bids on the same property, it may take the estate agent a while to let you know about future bids, so make regular contact with the estate agent, rather than waiting for him to contact you. Ask whether the bid is higher than yours, and if so, decide whether you are going to make a higher offer. But you must make sure that you are able to afford any offer that you make, and estate agents should take reasonable steps to ascertain the source and availability of funds for buying the property from prospective purchasers. Therefore, it is important that you decide upon a maximum price that you can afford before you make an offer on a property, and that you convince the estate agent that your offer is legitimate. Again, comprehensive price research is vital if you are to succeed in your bidding (see Chapter 6).

Completing on the sale

If you have made a bid on a property and it is the highest bid, you should try to complete as soon as possible, as other bids can be invited right up until the time that the contracts are exchanged. Once the exchange of contracts has taken place, both parties are legally bound to complete the transfer and they cannot pull out of the deal or accept higher bids from other buyers.

Bidding in Scotland

In Scotland, the house buying process can be seen to be much more robust, with little chance of gazumping. This is because, once a bid has been accepted and when the solicitors for both buyer and seller have reached agreement on the conditions of sale, the offer becomes legally binding on both the buyer and the seller. This means that neither can depart from the contract without the consent of the other.

In Scotland, sealed bids are made by your solicitor and all mortgages and surveys must be arranged before a bid is made. Although this system removes the problem of gazumping, it does mean that you may have to pay for a survey on every house in which you are interested until your bid is successful. (A single survey will be included in the home report (see Chapter 7) from December 2008). As solicitors play a much greater role in the house purchasing process, some people believe that there are fewer opportunities for estate agents to act unethically and unlawfully.

CASE STUDY 4: WENDY AND ANDY

Wendy and Andy found a house in their local town that had been repossessed. They knew the area well and felt that it would be a good place to live, especially as their family lived close by and Wendy was expecting her first baby. Wendy related her experience by email:

'We put in an offer and the estate agent told us that if our offer was accepted, it would have to be advertised for seven days. During this time, other people could make a higher offer. Then someone did put in a higher offer, but we didn't know how much for. Unfortunately, we'd already put in a fairly high offer because we wanted to try to stop other people bidding. This backfired on us when someone put in a higher offer. Eventually, we had to offer £5,000 more than our initial offer. It was accepted and we asked our solicitor to start the searches. Then we were told that the other interested party weren't happy and that they had wanted to put in another offer. So now we've both been told that we have to put in another offer. And, to make matters worse, we've been told to only put in offers that are £3,000 over the agreed offer as other offers will be disregarded.'

Wendy and Andy eventually lost the property because the other bidder put in an offer that they were unable to beat.

INCREASING YOUR CHANCES OF SUCCESS

In addition to the information offered above, you can increase your chances of success by taking notice of the following advice:

Sealed bids:

- Understand how much the property is worth and try to make a guess about how much others will offer. Speak to the estate agent and conduct a detailed price analysis to help you to know how much to bid (see Chapter 6). Also, try to find out more about the condition of the property before making your bid, as this will have an influence on the amount you offer. Consult the Home Information Pack (HIP) and ask builders or surveyors to look around the property and provide estimates for work (see Chapter 7).

- Make sure that you have your finances arranged before you make an offer and check that your lender will lend you sufficient finances to cover the amount that you wish to bid for the property.

- It is preferable to offer an odd amount, such as £150,001, as this will enable you to beat other people who have offered £150,000, for example. Also, remember to include the phrase 'subject to contract and without prejudice' on any written bid that you make, as this will help to protect you against problems that could arise before the exchange of contracts.

- Make sure that you act rapidly and that you can move quickly on the purchase. This will be harder to do if you are part of a chain and you have not found a buyer for your house. Check that your solicitor or conveyancer can deal with the paperwork as quickly as possible. The HIP (or home report in Scotland) should contain the required searches and documentation, so this should help you to move quicker (see Chapter 7). Remember to include information with your bid that illustrates that you can move quickly and that you are a serious buyer.

- Try to find out how many people are bidding against you. This will be easier to do if you build up a trusting relationship with the estate agent. Estate agents are under no obligation to tell you how many people are bidding, but some may offer this information 'off the record'.

- In some cases it is possible to make a further bid, even after the deadline, if you are not successful with your initial bid. This is a matter for your conscience – many sellers are willing to gazump, and this can work in your favour, but you must be happy with your actions if you choose this route. Also, if you use reputable agents (see page 112), they should not adopt this practice.

- Only use reputable agents and make sure that they are a member of a suitable redress scheme so that you can make a complaint if you feel they have acted unethically or unlawfully (see page 113).

Open bids:

- Monitor the local newspaper and speak to estate agents on a regular basis so that you can find out as soon as a repossessed property is advertised. This way you can act quickly and put in an offer as soon as possible. If the property is not widely advertised, you may be the only person to make a bid and, therefore, you could obtain the property at a bargain price. Also, on rare occasions, some notices of offer will indicate that the property is a repossession, and this may deter other buyers.

- Opinion is divided about whether you should be the first to make an initial low offer which is then advertised for seven or 14 days. This could mean that other people also make a low offer, which is only slightly above yours, and you then have leeway to raise your offer if required. Others feel it is better to make a higher bid from the outset in an attempt to deter other bidders. Some people believe that you are better waiting until someone else has made a bid, because you then have a better idea of how much to offer. The best advice is to do your research and use the method you find most preferable. Find out about local prices and how quickly properties are sold in the area. Find out how long the property has been on the market and whether there has been any other interest. At this present time the housing market is slowing and the number of repossessions is rising rapidly. This could provide the opportunity for you to make an uncontested offer on a bargain property.

- You should note that the time of year can make a difference. If you are able to put in an offer for a property at a time of year when people tend not to look for properties, such as over the Christmas period, you are more likely to be successful.

- Understand the bidding procedure. Make sure that you act quickly and keep in regular contact with the estate agent. Do not wait for him to contact you about higher bids, but telephone or visit on a regular basis. This will show that you are a keen purchaser and alert you quickly to any rival bids. Estate agents must let you know when someone has bid higher than your offer, so that you can bid again if you wish. They have to provide this information and they cannot discriminate against you in any way. If you believe that this is happening, you should raise your concerns with the manager. If the problems are not resolved, you may have to resort to making an official complaint (see page 113).

Once your bid has been accepted and the bidding procedure has been concluded, you could try asking the estate agent to remove the property from the market, and ask him to put this agreement in writing. Although the estate agent does not have to do this on your request, he may agree to do so if the lender is happy with the price you have offered and he believes that he will not receive a higher offer for the property.

MAKING SURE AGENTS ACT ETHICALLY AND LAWFULLY

Estate agents must comply with all laws relating to residential estate agency, including the Estate Agents Act 1979, the Property Misdescriptions Act 1991 and the Consumers, Estate Agents and Redress Act 2007 (see page 117 for more information about this Act). They must always act both within the law and in the best interests of their clients. But anecdotal evidence collected for this book reveals that this is not always the case. I have uncovered situations where estate agents are acting in their own interests, trying to maximise profit to the detriment of their clients. In some cases this action is unethical, and in some cases it is unlawful (see below). When you are buying a property through an estate agent, it is important that you understand your rights and know how estate agents should act. That way, you can challenge or report an estate agent that is not acting ethically and lawfully.

The important points of which you should be aware are listed below:

- By law, an estate agent must provide, in writing, confirmation of his instructions to act on your behalf in buying or selling a property. This must include details of fees, expenses and business terms. All phrases used, such as 'sole selling rights', must be clearly explained. ('Sole selling rights' means that you cannot use the services of another agent and if you sell the property yourself, you will still have to pay commission to the estate agent. The term 'multi-agency' may be preferable, as it means that you can have several agents working for you, but you only have to pay commission to the one who secures a sale. But you will pay more commission with this type of contract. Another phrase is 'sole agency', which means that the estate agent is entitled to commission if you sell your property to a buyer introduced to you by the estate agent within the period of your contract. You would also have to pay commission if you were to sell your property through another estate agent during this contract period. However, if you were to sell your property through your own efforts, you would not have to pay commission because you are not an estate agent.)

- An estate agent must tell you, immediately in writing, about any circumstances which may give rise to a conflict of interest. This includes situations where an employee and/or his relatives may own a property that is being sold or where he is trying to buy a property through the estate agents.

- An estate agent must not release confidential information that you have supplied without your permission.

- An estate agent must never deliberately misrepresent the value of a property in order to gain an instruction.

- Reasonable steps must be taken to ensure that all statements, whether written or oral, about a property are accurate and correct. All advertisements must be fair, decent and honest.

- All offers that are made on a property must be passed on to the vendor up until the contracts are exchanged, unless the vendor has requested that offers of a certain amount or type are not passed on. Once an offer has been made, the vendor can request that the property should be withdrawn from the market and the estate agent should do this as soon as he is instructed.

- An estate agent cannot discriminate against a potential purchaser in any way. This includes misrepresenting the nature of offers in preference for rival offers; failing to tell his client of an offer; giving details of properties first to those clients who have indicated that they would use other services from the estate agent; making it a condition that you must use other services provided by the agent.

- An estate agent must keep all potential purchasers informed of other offers that have been made on a property, although he does not have to pass on details of how much has been offered.

- An estate agent cannot act in a way that could be considered threatening or oppressive, or in a way that may cause harm, annoyance and/or alarm.

- An estate agent should not accept secret commissions, discounts, rebates or other profits from any person in connection with the affairs of a client, unless the details have been disclosed to the client.

Making a complaint

If you believe that an estate agent has acted unethically or unlawfully, you should approach him first to find out whether the problem can be resolved.

All complaints should be acknowledged within seven working days and you should be provided with a formal written outcome within 21 days, unless you have been informed in writing that the investigation will take longer.

If you cannot come to an agreement with the estate agent, you can register your complaint with either the National Association of Estate Agents (NAEA) or the Ombudsman for Estate Agents (OEA), if the estate agent is a member. If you choose to make a complaint to the NAEA, the association will investigate your complaint and take action if required. A breach of the rules by a member can result in a caution, reprimand, fine, reclassification of membership, suspension or expulsion.

In certain cases you may be unhappy with the way an estate agent has acted, even though he has not breached the rules of the NAEA. If this is the case, you may be able to take advantage of the NAEA mediation service. This service is available to everyone and avoids problems associated with expensive and lengthy legal battles. A mediator is appointed who has the power to recommend a refund of commission, fees or other expenses, although this service does not make arrangements for compensation payments.

The OEA, on the other hand, is able to award for financial compensation and if you choose to accept this award, you do so in full and final settlement of your dispute. Unlike the NAEA, the work of the Ombudsman is to compensate you for any disadvantage you may have suffered. It is not to punish the agent and the Ombudsman has no remit to impose fines or serve other types of punishment on estate agents. More information about making a complaint can be obtained from the NAEA or OEA (contact details are provided in Appendix 2: Useful Organisations).

QUESTIONABLE PRACTICES

During the research for this book, I have come across a number of questionable practices by some estate agents. As mentioned above, some of these are unethical and some are unlawful.

In Chapter 5 it was pointed out that I approached seven estate agents in my local town, posing as a buyer and asking about repossessed properties, but only one estate agent gave me details about a property that had been repossessed, although one indicated that he had some 'distress sales' on his books. When I was speaking to a local property developer, and told him that estate agents seemed reluctant to pass on details about repossessed properties, he laughed and said that this did not surprise him. When I asked why, he said that it is very difficult for the normal house purchaser to find out about repossessed properties because estate agents keep the details of this type of property for their 'pet developers'. These are people who will pay a 'finder's fee', which will be anything between one to three per cent (in cash), to estate agents when they introduce them to suitable development opportunities. He pointed out that the larger, corporate estate agents will not enter into this type of deal, because it is a 'dodgy practice', but that property developers can soon find the 'shady' estate agents who will do this type of deal.

Property developers, according to my source, can find the right estate agents by visiting them, talking to them, taking them out to dinner and 'sussing them out'. These developers have their 'pet estate agents' whom they will approach for properties. It is an unwritten rule, he said, that if property developers are able to buy a property cheaply through an estate agent, they will then use that estate agent to resell the property, once it has been converted. He told me that, as a property developer, you 'feel obliged' to do this because the estate agent has helped you to find a bargain property. 'Dodgy' estate agents are happy to undertake this practice because they can obtain a quick sale, they do not need to advertise their property, and they will receive two sets of commission when the property is put back on the market.

The property developer had bought over 20 repossessions, and, although he was reluctant to admit that he undertook this practice, it seemed that he was hinting that this was the case. (See Chapter 3 (page 29) for a quotation from a property investor who did admit to undertaking this practice.) Despite benefiting from this type of relationship with estate agents, this developer said that he tends not to trust them. Unfortunately, he has to deal with estate agents as he is unable to contact the lender direct. In an ideal world, he says, he would contact lenders himself and cut out the 'middle man'.

Official response

I contacted the NAEA, which is now part of the National Federation of

Property Professionals, to find out its view on such practices, and I received the following reply:

> *'Dear Dr. Dawson*
>
> *Thank you for your enquiry.*
>
> *If the agent is receiving payment from the vendor and the developer who is purchasing the property, then this could potentially be in breach of the law of agency as the agent can only have one paying client.*
>
> *Failure to market the property properly on the open market may also not be in the client's interests, as it may mean that the client does not obtain the best possible price for the property.*
>
> *Discrimination against particular purchasers may also be in breach of the Estate Agents Act 1979.*
>
> *I can understand why agents do not inform potential purchasers of property that may have been repossessed, or which is a distress sale, because it may not be in the client's best interests in obtaining the best possible price for the property.'*
>
> **National Federation of Property Professionals, January 2008, Warwick.**

This response makes it clear that accepting a cash finder's fee from property developers is not a lawful practice. If you believe that an estate agent in your area is undertaking this practice, you should consider making a complaint in the manner described above or to your local Trading Standards office. You can find the Trading Standards office nearest to you by entering your postcode on its website (www.trading standards.gov.uk). Interestingly, the issue is viewed slightly differently from a lender's point of view:

> *'Lenders are under a duty to find the best price that can reasonably be obtained and this [practice] would only be an issue from a lender's perspective if it was circumventing this.'*
>
> **Email from the Council of Mortgage Lenders (CML), 12 March 2008.**

AUTHOR'S NOTE

When I obtain information for my research, I assure the people that I am interviewing that the information will only be used for the stated purpose (in this case, to include in my book). Also, I will not use names and addresses, unless they are happy for me to do so. Although I uncovered these unlawful practices taking place locally, I feel I cannot report the information or make an official complaint, because this would breach my researcher's Code of Ethics. I would feel differently, however, if this happened when I was trying to a buy a repossessed property, rather than during my research.

The Consumers, Estate Agents and Redress Act 2007

An awareness of the Consumers, Estate Agents and Redress Act 2007 is important if you feel that you have encountered problems with an estate agent. Part of this Act is an amendment of the Estate Agents Act 1979 and has been introduced to improve redress in the estate agent sector. This should help to protect you, as the customer, and it will enable you to seek redress against an estate agent who has treated you unfairly. The relevant part of the Act covers the following issues:

- Estate agents' duties:

    - Estate agents must join an approved redress scheme, which will be used to handle complaints against estate agents made by people buying and selling residential property.

    - Estate agents will be required to keep adequate records of their dealings with a client for six years.

- Prohibition and warning orders:

    - The Office of Fair Trading (OFT) has more scope to consider an estate agent's fitness to practise.

    - The OFT and Trading Standards will be able to inspect an estate agent's files when it is deemed necessary.

- Investigatory powers:

    - Enforcement authorities have increased powers to enter premises and seize documents if they have reasonable cause to suspect that an offence has been committed under this Act.

As these points illustrate, this part of the Act should make it easier for you to make a complaint and for this complaint to be investigated by the enforcement authorities. More detailed information about this Act can be obtained from the Department for Business, Enterprise and Regulatory Reform (BERR) (www.berr.gov.uk).

Beating the property developers

If you are able to make a complaint, questionable practices in your area may be investigated and estate agents may be warned about their practices. This could help to stop property developers from beating the ordinary buyer to the best bargains. However, some complaints may not be investigated, or may take considerable time, and, in other cases, estate agents may continue to adopt these practices.

If this is the case, you need to beat the property developers at their own game. To do this, you will need to build up a network of reliable estate agents and get yourself known to them. Visit regularly and engage in conversation about local property bargains that are coming onto the market. Make it clear that you are interested in buying a repossession and emphasise any advantages you might have, such as being a cash buyer or having a pre-arranged mortgage. Speak to different people in the office at different times so that you can get your face and name known amongst the staff. Spread your net wide – register with all the estate agents in the area, face-to-face and online.

Get your name on the mailing list of all auction houses in the area and visit some local auctions, even if you are not interested in a specific property. This will help you to understand the buying process and it may help you to recognise some of the property developers who are operating in the area. Take note of their tactics at auction, and if they appear to be successful, adopt similar tactics yourself.

More information about beating the competition is offered in Chapter 5.

SUMMARY

When you are buying a repossessed property through an estate agent, it is important to understand the advertising and bidding procedure, so that you can act quickly when a property becomes available. Once an offer has been made on a property, many estate agents will place a 'notice of offer' in the local newspaper. Sealed or open bids will be invited, and, in some cases, this will be up until contracts are exchanged. Therefore, you will increase your chances of success if you can move quickly on the purchase. It is important that you maintain regular contact with the estate agent and make sure that he is acting ethically and lawfully. If you suspect malpractice, you can consider making a complaint.

Many repossessed properties are offered for sale by auction, rather than through an estate agent. There are different procedures that need to be adopted if you decide to purchase a repossessed property through auction and these are discussed in the following chapter.

CHAPTER 9:
BUYING REPOSSESSED PROPERTY AT AUCTION

'It was quite scary because I've never done that sort of thing before. But my brother went with me and helped. He told me to watch for phantom bids, which he said are bids made by the person who is selling the property. They wouldn't do that, would they? Is that allowed? Anyway, I didn't get the house because it was sold for too much. My brother told me not to get carried away and I didn't.'

Jamie, Northampton.

Research conducted by the Royal Institution of Chartered Surveyors (RICS) reports that the number of residential properties offered at auction rose by 32 per cent in the second quarter of 2007. The highest concentration of auction activity was in the North West of England, where 826 residential properties were sold through auction in the second quarter. This part of the country has also witnessed a steep rise in the number of repossession orders over the last year. Since RICS predicts that repossessions will continue to climb higher into 2008 and could exceed 45,000, it seems inevitable that the number of residential properties offered at auction will continue to increase significantly. At present, up to 90 per cent of cheap homes sold in the UK are sold through auction, according to First Rung Now, the website aimed at first-time buyers (www.firstrungnow.com).

If you are hoping to obtain a bargain repossessed property at auction, it is important to understand how auctions work, how to arrange adequate finance, how to make sure that the property is suitable and how to bid without getting carried away. These issues are discussed in this chapter.

'When a property goes to auction it is because lenders believe that this will fetch the best price for it. They make this decision in consultation with their estate agent, based on the condition of the individual property and local market conditions. Anecdotally, we know that the majority of properties are still sold through estate agents.'

Email from the Council of Mortgage Lenders (CML), 12 March 2008.

UNDERSTANDING HOW AUCTIONS WORK

Properties that are to be sold at auction can be advertised in several ways. If the auction house works closely with local estate agents, the property will be advertised by the agent in the usual way. This can include information in the window of the premises, an advert in the local paper and property details on the agent's website. If an auctioneer is marketing the property, it will be advertised in the auction catalogue and it may appear in the local press.

As we have seen previously, some lenders do not wish the auction house to advertise the property as a repossession. Others, however, provide this information by including any of the following phrases in the catalogue:

- By order of the mortgagee.

- By order of the mortgagees in possession.

- On behalf of mortgagees in possession.

- By order of…Building Society.

- On the instruction of an LPA Receiver. (This is a person who is appointed, under the Law of Property Act 1925, to take charge of a mortgaged property by a lender whose loan is in default – see Glossary of Terms.)

- On the instructions of a liquidator.

Knowing about price

The property will be advertised with a 'guide price'. This gives an indication of the price that the property is expected to sell for and what the vendor is hoping to achieve. In some cases, this will have been decided upon by the estate agent; in other cases, by the auctioneer or by the lender that is selling the property. This price should be a realistic price, although it may be a little below the market value of the property to attract interest.

Some lenders will set a 'reserve price', which is the minimum price for which the property can be sold. The level at which this reserve price is set will depend on a number of factors, including the amount of time the property has been on the market, the current market valuation of similar properties in the area and the condition of the property. As we have seen previously, lenders are under a 'duty of care' to ensure that they obtain the best possible price for the property, but they also need to sell the property as quickly as possible. Some, therefore, will set a low reserve price, whereas others will set a higher reserve price and some may choose not to set a reserve price at all. Auction houses will also offer an auction appraisal of the property and provide advice on a recommended reserve price.

'The number of repossessions should continue rising in 2008 as the full effects of interest rate rises feed through into higher effective mortgage rates, i.e. the rate of interest passed on from the base rate into the mortgage markets. Homeowners, coming to the end of fixed-rate deals, will see a jump in mortgage servicing costs, having been sheltered over the last year as interest rates have risen. As such, residential lots offered at auction should continue to pick up with RICS estimating that repossessions could rise in excess of 45,000 in 2008. This would represent an annualised rise of 50 per cent in repossessions from current levels in 2008, although it would still be only around half that experienced in the early 1990s. While the number of lots offered will continue to grow, an easing in demand pressure in the general housing market should lead to a moderation in success rates into 2008. Buying at auction will

remain appealing to investors who are looking to take advantage of a quick turnaround time for property purchasing.'

RICS, 'The Auction Market', 2007.

Finding out about auctions

To find out about local auctions in your area, visit local estate agents and ask for details. If they work with auction houses, they will provide contact details and information about how you can be put on the mailing list. Once this has been done, you will receive regular catalogues for forthcoming sales. Properties that are to be sold through auction need to be registered at least six weeks beforehand so that the auctioneer has time to include details in the latest catalogue and market the property appropriately. This should give you enough time to view properties that you are interested in.

A list of members of the National Association of Estate Agents (NAEA) who are involved in auctions specialising in residential and commercial property can be obtained from www.naea.co.uk/auctions. This database provides the name of the auctioneer, the date and time of the next auction, the closing date for bookings, the address, the telephone/fax number and email address of the auctioneer. If you choose to use an auctioneer that is a member of the NAEA, you can be sure that you are dealing with an experienced and professional auctioneer who has to abide by the NAEA Rules of Conduct (see Chapter 8).

Making an offer prior to the auction

If you find a suitable property, it is possible to make an offer prior to the auction. This offer must be reasonable and, if so, it will be forwarded to the lender who will decide whether or not to accept the offer. If it does accept the offer, your purchase can go ahead. But, in most cases, the property will only be withdrawn from the auction when the contracts have been exchanged, so if you decide upon this route, you will need to move quickly on your purchase. Also, it is possible for other people to make higher offers on the property until contracts are exchanged, so, again, the quicker you can move on the purchase, the better your chances of success.

ARRANGING FINANCE

When you buy a property at auction, you must make sure that you have enough money available for a deposit on the day of the sale. This is usually ten per cent of the sale price or a minimum stated figure, whichever is the greater. You can use the guide price to help you to estimate how much this deposit is likely to be. Also, you will need to have your mortgage arranged prior to the auction so that you can go ahead with the purchase in the timescale required, which is usually within 28 days. Do not be tempted to bid at auction if you have not got all the required finances in place, as the balance of the sale will need to be paid on completion.

Before you make a bid at auction for a repossessed property, there are other expenses that you will have to take into consideration when you are arranging your finances. These are described below.

Solicitor's/conveyancer's fees

You will need to obtain the services of a solicitor before you go to auction so that he can look through the paperwork and advise you on any legal issues of which you should be aware before you bid on the property. Solicitor's and conveyancer's fees vary, but they could be in the range of £600–£1,200, depending on the work you require and the size and type of property in which you are interested. To find a solicitor in your area, visit the Law Society's website (www.lawsociety.org.uk). To find a licensed conveyancer in your area, use the online directory on the website of the Council for Licensed Conveyancers (www.conveyancer.org.uk).

Surveyor's fees

You will need to make sure that a survey is arranged on the property prior to the date of auction. The different types of survey are described in Chapter 7. Prices vary, depending on the type of survey and the size of the property, but they should be in the region of £300–£1,000. Unfortunately, you will have to pay these fees, regardless of whether you are successful in obtaining the property at auction.

Stamp Duty Land Tax

Stamp Duty Land Tax (SDLT) is payable on the purchase of land and buildings in the UK, and it can add a significant cost to the purchase of a property. You will need to make sure that you have this money available before you decide to buy at auction.

But SDLT is only payable on residential properties costing more than £125,000 and there is relief available for transactions in disadvantaged areas. You can find out whether a property in which you are interested qualifies for Disadvantaged Areas Relief (DAR) by using the search tool available on HM Revenue & Customs' (HMRC) website (www.hmrc. gov.uk). Current SDLT rates are provided in the table below. For up-to-date rates, visit HMRC's website.

STAMP DUTY LAND TAX RATES (2008/09)

Rates	Residential Land in Disadvantaged Areas	All Other Residential Land in the UK	All Other Non-Residential Land in the UK
Zero	£0–£150,000	£0–£125,000	£0–£150,000
1%	Over £150,000–£250,000	Over £125,000–£250,000	Over £150,000–£250,000
3%	Over £250,000–£500,000	Over £250,000–£500,000	Over £250,000–£500,000
4%	Over £500,000	Over £500,000	Over £500,000

Mortgage fees

When you arrange a mortgage, in most cases, you will need to pay an administration fee, which could be in the region of £100–£500. If you decide to use a mortgage broker, you may have a fee of up to £300 to pay, although some mortgage brokers will receive commission from the mortgage company instead of a fee from their client. If the property that you buy at auction is in need of modernisation or renovation, you may have to pay a re-inspection fee if the mortgage company withholds some of your loan until you carry out agreed repairs to the property. This could be up to £250.

Contact your chosen lender for more information about its fees. You should do this before the auction takes place, so you will know how much you have to pay for your mortgage before you bid on a property.

VIEWING THE PROPERTY

It is advisable that you arrange to view the property at least twice, if possible, prior to the auction. Comprehensive information and advice about viewing a property is provided in Chapter 7. It is important to give yourself plenty of time when you are undertaking these viewings, so that you can return to the property with experts and/or surveyors if you need to seek expert advice on any problems that you have found. If major work is required, obtain quotations from relevant professionals, so that you have a clear idea about how much you will need to spend on the property. This will help you to understand how much you can realistically offer for the property at auction.

'I found it really intimidating visiting the property with loads of other people. They really seemed to know what they were doing and it was a bit scary for me because I just didn't know what I was doing. My brother said that next time I should ask if they would let me go on my own. He says some will let you do that if you ask.'

Jamie, Northampton.

Some auction houses will arrange special days for viewing property prior to the auction and details of these will appear in their catalogue. But you should also try to view the property at a day and time that suits you and many auction houses will let you do this, subject to prior arrangement. If the property has been advertised through an estate agent, he will arrange for you to undertake a viewing and he will accompany you when you look around the property. If a property is tenanted, there may be restrictions placed on the number and timing of viewings.

ARRANGING A SURVEY

All surveys will need to be conducted before the date of the auction and you will need to make sure that they are carried out in good time so that you can inspect the report and commission further specialist surveys, if required. Some lenders will include a Home Condition Report (HCR) in their Home Information Pack (HIP), although this is not a compulsory component of the pack. In most cases, it is advisable that you commission your own survey for the property, as this can alert you to potential and costly problems. This is of particular importance if the property is dilapidated, in a poor state of repair, or has been deliberately damaged. To obtain contact details of a surveyor in your area, use the online directory at www.ricsfirms.com. More information about arranging a survey is provided in Chapter 7.

PREPARING FOR THE AUCTION

There are several things that you need to do when you are preparing for an auction, as detailed below:

- Make sure that you have a deposit of at least ten per cent of the guide price available for the day of the auction (see page 125).

- Make sure that you have your mortgage agreement in place before the day of the auction.

- Check that the structure of the property is sound and that there are no other expensive problems by consulting the survey report that you have already commissioned.

- Consult a solicitor about the purchase as this will help you to avoid any legal pitfalls.

- Check a copy of the legal documents that will be available from the auctioneer.

- Make sure that you have a copy of the auction catalogue as 'the memorandum' printed within the catalogue forms part of the legal contract between you and the seller. If you buy a property at auction, you sign your copy and exchange this with the lender's signed copy. The copy that you receive then acts as a receipt for the deposit you have paid on the day.

- Find out the location of the auction venue in advance. Check to see whether there are any problems with roadworks or delays on public transport which may cause you to be late or miss the bidding on your chosen property. Find out about ease of parking. Contact the auction house to find out whether it is likely to be busy and whether parking in the area may be a problem. Work out how long the journey takes so that you can arrive in good time and so you can find a suitable place to sit or stand.

- When you go to the auction you will need to take the following:

    - Two forms of identification.

    - Your auction catalogue.

    - Your solicitor's details.

    - Your deposit, which can be a banker's draft, a building society cheque, cash or a personal cheque.

- You may have to be prepared to pay a 'contract documentation fee' (a fee to cover the cost of the auction process), which is usually in the region of £150–£200 or 'administration' fees, which could be in the region of £150–£300. Ask the auction house for details about costs prior to the auction.

KNOWING HOW TO BID

Before bidding begins, the auctioneer will check that everybody has a copy of the 'Addendum' or 'Announcement' sheet, and he will read out any last-minute alterations to the catalogue's details. You will need to check the sheet and listen carefully to make sure that there are no alterations to the details of the property in which you are interested.

Your background research and the availability of your finances will enable you to understand how much you are able to bid. Write this figure on a piece of paper or on the back of your hand to remind yourself that this is the maximum you can bid. You may find it useful to take a sensible friend or relative with you and instruct him to make sure that you do not exceed this amount.

Listen carefully for your property and be prepared to make a bid when it comes up. Do not jump in immediately with a bid, but wait to see what happens. Experienced bidders do this in the hope that an auctioneer will reduce the starting price and if there are no other bidders, they will receive an exceptional bargain. Once a bid has been made, you can enter the bidding process. Do this slowly at first – you do not want to appear to be too keen, if possible.

AUTHOR'S NOTE

We have bought quite a few of our properties at auction over the years. It is interesting to note how auctions have changed over this time. Initially, they were frequented by property developers, investors and landlords and we used to recognise many faces from our local landlord's group. But over recent years they are frequented much more by the ordinary buyer who is looking for a home. Interestingly, property developers, landlords and investors seem to be staying away and there are fewer familiar faces present.

A property developer who was interviewed for this book said it was to do with the increase in television programmes and books about property auctions. This has led to ordinary homebuyers frequenting auctions and prices have been pushed up, partly, he thinks, due to inexperience and lack of knowledge from bidders. He believes this has led to many property developers and investors choosing not to buy at auction because there are fewer bargains available. However, we find that this is not necessarily the case – at certain auctions prices have indeed been pushed up, but at others we are still able to obtain properties at bargain prices.

Accidental bids

It is a common misconception that you can accidentally make a bid at an auction by scratching your nose or sneezing, for example. This is not the case – auctioneers ask that you make a bid clearly, by your raising either your hand or a copy of the auction catalogue, while you are making eye contact with the auctioneer. Experienced auctioneers can recognise instantly when someone has made a bid and they can remember who has bid, where they are sitting or standing, and they know when to return to you to find out whether you intend to bid further. If the price has gone too high for you, make it clear that you no longer intend to bid by shaking your head when the auctioneer looks at you to invite a further bid.

'I offered £2,000 over the guide price before the sale. I was too scared to go to auction – I thought I might accidentally buy ten properties or something. What a nightmare that would be! Luckily, there didn't seem to be any more interest, so I got the house and it was withdrawn because we completed two weeks before the sale.'

Jo, Plymouth.

Exchange of contracts

Once you have made the final bid and it has been accepted, this becomes the 'exchange of contracts' and you cannot pull out of the completion. But this means that you cannot be gazumped by someone offering a higher bid at a later stage. This is of particular importance when you are buying a repossessed property as the person who has been evicted may be able to put a stop on the sale right up until the completion date, when you use other channels (see Chapter 2). Also, it removes much of the stress that can occur with the bidding procedure adopted by estate agents (see Chapter 8).

Non-attendance

If you are unable to attend the auction, or you feel that you are not experienced enough to bid yourself, you can arrange to bid by telephone or arrange for someone else to bid for you. If you choose to make a telephone bid, a member of the auction team will be in the auction room to make your bid as instructed by you over the telephone. If you decide to ask someone from the auction team to make bids on your behalf, you will need to arrange this at least two days before the day of the auction. A member of the auction team will need your written consent to act on your behalf and you will need to make sure that he is informed of your maximum limit. In certain cases, you may be able to bid over the internet – the auction catalogue will contain information about whether this is possible and if so, the procedure you will need to follow.

CASE STUDY 5: GEORGINA

Georgina had been trying to step onto the property ladder for a considerable amount of time, but, as she was on a low income, she was finding it impossible. Eventually, her parents decided that they would help her to do this by offering to pay the deposit on a property. But Georgina knew that she had to look for the cheapest type of property in the area if she was not going to stretch herself too much, financially, each month.

During a visit to a local estate agent, she obtained details of a property that was to be auctioned in two months' time. Georgina had not thought about buying a property at auction, but when she showed the details to her parents they felt that the opportunity was too good to be missed. They returned to the estate agent, who told them more about the auction procedure and gave them a booklet called 'Buying and Selling at a Property Auction'. This booklet provided a step-by-step guide to the whole procedure and they felt that it prepared them well. The estate agent acknowledged that the property was a repossession, when he was pushed by Georgina's father.

They went to visit the property, taking along Georgina's brother who was a builder. He inspected the structure of the property and, although he was not an expert, he felt that it was sound. The parents checked everything else they could think of and felt that the property could represent a bargain, if it was sold around the guide price. They visited the property a second time and arranged for a survey to be undertaken.

The only stumbling block was when Georgina tried to arrange a mortgage. Unfortunately, her annual wage was not enough for the amount she needed to borrow. The only option was for her parents to act as guarantors, which meant that although Georgina was named on the mortgage, the amount that she could borrow was based on the income of her parents, thus enabling her to borrow more. Her parents felt that they would be able to release themselves from the mortgage when Georgina was earning enough to support the loan.

At the auction, Georgina's father undertook the bidding as he was concerned that Georgina may have got carried away. They were successful in obtaining the property at £5,000 above the guide price, which was within their budget. Everybody in the family was happy and Georgina was able to move into her new home a few weeks later. She felt that she had been extremely lucky, first, to have parents who were willing to help her financially and, second, to have obtained a lovely property at a reasonable price.

Since moving in Georgina has not experienced any problems with debt collectors, bailiffs or the previous owners.

SUMMARY

Experts believe that the number of repossessions offered at auction will increase significantly over the next few years. Some lenders prefer not to make it known that the property is a repossession, whereas others provide this information in the catalogue. If you intend to buy at auction, you need to make sure that you have undertaken a thorough viewing, you have arranged your finances and you have prepared well for the auction, taking with you all the necessary documentation. You may find it useful to take a trusted friend or relative with you who can make sure that you do not bid more than you can afford. It is possible to arrange for someone to bid for you if you are unable to attend the auction.

Once you have been successful in obtaining your repossessed property, whether through auction or through an estate agent, you will be able to complete the buying process and move into your new home. There are certain issues that you should be aware of when you are moving into a repossessed property. These issues are discussed in the following chapter.

FURTHER READING

Comprehensive advice about all aspects of buying property at auction can be obtained from the following book, which has been written by a freelance auctioneer.

Gooddie, H R (2007), *Buying Bargains at Property Auctions*, 4th edition, London: Lawpack Publishing Ltd. (This book is available from www. lawpack.co.uk.)

CHAPTER 10:

UNDERSTANDING THE CONVEYANCING PROCESS

'The solicitors for the lender will always provide the usual response in their standard response to enquiries, i.e. the seller has not lived at the property and therefore has no knowledge and the buyer must rely on his own searches and enquiries. It is, therefore, important that all searches are carried out insofar as the buyer will permit (many are on a budget, first-time buyers, etc., but it is important to point out to them the importance of all searches). No specific damage has to be placed in the pre-contract information.'

A P Malam Property Lawyers, Conwy.

Once you have made an offer on a repossessed property, the conveyancing process can begin. This is the legal procedure involved in transferring buildings and/or land from one owner to another and dealing with the financial transactions. In Scotland, the conveyancing process begins before bids are made on a property (see page 144); whereas in England and Wales it begins once an offer has been made. It includes the searches described in the quotation above and it will ascertain that the title to the property (the legal basis of ownership of a property) is in order and it will check on possible neighbour/boundary disputes or any problems that may have arisen from the survey. Also included will be a property information form and a fixtures and fitting form that details what will be included in the sale.

Checks will be made on the financial arrangements, making sure that you have all the necessary finances and that you can pay the deposit when required and that you have a suitable mortgage in place. These issues are discussed in this chapter.

APPOINTING A CONVEYANCER

The conveyancing process is carried out by a solicitor or a conveyancer. In certain circumstances, it can be undertaken by you, as the buyer. But if you intend to undertake the conveyancing process yourself, you must make sure that you understand the process and that you have the necessary skills and knowledge. Also, some solicitors acting for the lender that is selling the repossessed property may be reluctant to deal with someone who is not a fully qualified conveyancer. If this is the case, you will need to appoint a qualified person to act for you. As buying a repossession can be a complex process, it is advisable that you make sure that you have an experienced and competent person who is able to undertake the process for you.

The Council for Licensed Conveyancers (CLC) is the regulatory body for licensed conveyancers who are trained and qualified in all aspects of the law dealing with property. You can find a conveyancer by using the online directory on the CLC's website (www.conveyancer.org.uk). You can search the directory by name, town or county, or by clicking on the map of England and Wales. Licensed conveyancers do not operate in Scotland; instead, conveyancing work is carried out by qualified solicitors.

 *'Licensed conveyancers are required to comply with the regulatory requirements, which include maintaining professional indemnity insurance and compliance with all the rules of professional conduct, including the timely disclosure of relevant information to clients, such as cost estimates, financial arrangements with third parties and updates on key developments in the matter.*

All the key parties involved in the home buying and selling process, including financial institutions such as banks and lenders, recognise licensed conveyancers.'

The Council for Licensed Conveyancers, 2008.

If you prefer to use a solicitor to carry out the conveyancing process, use the Law Society's website to find a solicitor in your area (www.lawsociety. org.uk). You can search the directory by area of law (conveyancing residential), firm name, postcode, location and country. If you are buying and selling at the same time, it makes financial sense and it will be more efficient to use the same person to conduct both conveyances. If you live in Scotland, you can find a solicitor by contacting the Law Society of Scotland (www.lawscot.org.uk).

Costs

Solicitor and conveyancer fees vary, but may be in the range of £600–£1,200, depending on the work you require, the size and type of property in which you are interested and whether any problems are encountered during the searches or investigation of title (see below). Some solicitors and conveyancers will offer an individual quotation based on a preliminary discussion, whereas others will provide a standard price as a guide to costs. They will lay out these costs in a letter, which you must then sign and return if you wish to use their services. A final breakdown of your services and costs will be sent to you for payment before completion. You should note that your solicitor or conveyancer will also arrange for Stamp Duty Land Tax (SDLT) to be paid after completion – see Chapter 9 for the current rates.

CARRYING OUT SEARCHES

During the conveyancing process, searches are undertaken on the property to make sure that there is nothing that will have an adverse influence on your property purchase, such as proposed highway development or compulsory purchase orders. These give public authorities, such as the local authority or National Park Authority, and statutory corporations, such as the Environment Agency and the Civil Aviation Authority, the power to acquire land and buildings. They may do this to clear unfit housing for development and regeneration, or for a new highway or airport expansion, for example.

Standard searches will be included in the Home Information Pack (HIP) (paid for by the seller) and your solicitor or conveyancer will check these and offer advice about whether other searches should be undertaken, and if so, how much they will cost you. The search process may include the following:

- **Local searches** – these relate to the property and they will check the following:

    - If there is a road widening scheme or there are any other compulsory orders in place which may affect the property.

    - If the building has listed status.

    - If the road outside the property is publicly maintained.

    - If the property is subject to any planning permissions or tree preservation orders.

    - If the property has problems with hedgerows.

    - If there has been any breach of building regulations or planning controls on the property and whether any action is being taken by the local authority.

    - If there are any potential development plans in the area that could affect the property's value.

- **Environment searches** – these will check environment factors, such as the following:

    - Local mining works that could affect the stability of the property.

    - Problems with subsidence in the area.

    - Problems with contaminated land.

    - Problems with radon gas.

    - The property being located on a flood plain or in other areas in which flooding could be possible.

    - Problems with pollution or noise.

Information for searches is obtained from local authorities and from electronic conveyancing search services, such as the National Land Information Service (NLIS) (www.nlis.org.uk), SearchFlow (www.search flow.co.uk) or Jordans Property (www.jordansproperty.co.uk). In 2006 a Search Code was introduced that should help to protect you, as a buyer, against misleading or incorrect information provided in searches. This code includes a code of conduct for both compliers and retailers of search reports. More information about this code can be obtained from the Property Codes Compliance Board (www.propertycodes.org.uk).

If you have requested that additional searches be undertaken, other than those included in the HIP, the information will be forwarded to you. Occasionally, your solicitor, or conveyancer, may advise you that the problem uncovered by the searches will have an adverse influence on your purchase and he may advise you to pull out of the purchase. This could occur, for example, if the property is located on a flood plain that has been shown to have flooded in the past or in cases where mining works have caused severe subsidence to neighbouring properties.

There can be risks associated with buying any property, but perhaps more so with a repossession that may not have been as well maintained as other properties may have been. For example, a person who is struggling financially may be tempted to employ 'cowboys' to build an extension, or even decide to do the work himself, without the necessary qualifications or planning permissions. This information may not be readily available in the HIP and searches carried out by your conveyancer or solicitor would uncover this type of problem and alert you to the financial costs and legal implications. Therefore, you should try to make sure that you can afford all the necessary searches that may be required, in addition to those provided in the HIP.

CHECKING TITLE DEEDS

During the conveyancing process the title deeds of the property will be checked to make sure that the person selling the property is actually able to do so. While it is the lender who is selling the property after repossession, it is the borrower who is still legally the owner. Your solicitor, or conveyancer, will check that the voluntary possession declaration or legal paperwork from the courts are in order (see Chapter 2), and he will check that the evicted borrower is the person named on the title deeds.

This investigation of title will also check rights of way over the property and covenants, which may include issues such as erecting satellite dishes and business use of the property. If there are any restrictions placed on the property, your solicitor or conveyancer will check that this does not conflict with your proposed use for the property.

Types of title

There are different levels of title in England and Wales and these are described below, so that you can understand the potential pitfalls that may be present. But since the property has been repossessed by the lender, there must have been a mortgage on the property, and most lenders would not have granted a mortgage in the first place if there was a problem with the title to the property.

Absolute title

An 'absolute title' or 'title absolute' is the best title that the Land Registry can give land and if this is the type of title on the property you are hoping to buy, you should not encounter any further problems with the title.

Qualified title

In certain cases, there may be defects in the legal documents that cause concern. This is known as a 'qualified title', but can also be referred to as a 'defect title' or 'defective title'. It can occur when documents are missing, destroyed, lost or simply inadequate. Your solicitor, or conveyancer, may advise you to pull out of the sale because the problem cannot be rectified, or he may advise you to obtain 'defective title insurance', which will protect you, or your lender, against any financial loss that could occur as a result of the defective title. This type of insurance is normally provided at the seller's expense.

Possessory title

Some properties may have what is called a 'possessory title'. This could occur, for example, where the title deeds have been lost, but where a person has possession of the property. In this case the Land Registry is not entirely satisfied as to the vendor's ownership of the property, but is satisfied that the person is in lawful possession. Your solicitor, or conveyancer, will check for how long the possessory title has been held and, if it is over ten years (for registered land) or 12 years (for unregistered land), he will suggest that the vendor upgrades to an absolute title before you buy the property. It is also possible to take out a Title Indemnity Policy to protect against any adverse claims made in respect of the property. In extreme cases ,there may be discrepancies that cannot be resolved and your solicitor, or conveyancer, may recommend pulling out of the deal.

Absolute leasehold and good leasehold

If the property that you are buying is leasehold, there are two main classes of title – 'absolute leasehold title' and 'good leasehold'. 'Absolute leasehold title' means that the freehold title is registered and that the Land Registry can guarantee the title of the freeholder (the title owned by the landlord) and, therefore, it has the right to grant the lease. 'Good leasehold' means that the freeholder's title is not registered and is therefore not guaranteed by the Land Registry. In this case, the Land Registry limits the title granted to the leaseholder (which will be you, if you buy the property). The title is 'good', unless it turns out, at a later stage, that the apparent landlord did not have the right to grant the lease. If the property that you are intending to buy is 'good leasehold', your solicitor, or conveyancer, will need to obtain certified evidence of the freehold title. If he is unable to do this, you may be advised to pull out of the sale.

Types of ownership

Your solicitor, or conveyancer, will check the type of ownership on the property and make sure that you understand the implications for your purchase. In England and Wales there are three types of ownership, as detailed below. This information should be available in the HIP, but you may wish to ask the selling agent further questions to clarify the situation, if you are in doubt. It is useful to know about the type of ownership because it has implications for what you can do to a property, such as erect a satellite dish, keep pets or build extensions.

Freehold

With this type of ownership, the householder owns both the property and the land on which it is built. This is the most flexible type of ownership and there should be fewer restrictions on what you can do with your property in terms of development, as a freehold gives the buyer the right to do as he likes with his home, subject to the law and planning controls. If you are buying a repossessed freehold property, there will not be any problems with arrears on ground rent or service charges.

Leasehold

With this type of ownership, the householder owns the property for a set number of years, but he does not own the land on which it stands. Flats and houses can be leasehold, although this type of ownership is much more common in flats. Leasehold flats can be in purpose-built blocks, in converted houses, or above commercial or retail premises. The ownership of the flat tends to relate to everything within the flat, but it usually does not include the external or structural walls. Instead, the structure and common parts of the building and the land it stands on are owned by the freeholder, who is responsible for the maintenance and repair of the building.

Leasehold is a tenancy which means that you will have to pay a ground rent, although this may be nominal. You may also have to pay a service charge and you should ask how much this charge has been over the years and how much it is likely to be in the future, as it can change from year to year. If you are buying a repossessed flat that is leasehold, you should check that there are no outstanding debts on ground rent and that no service charges have been left by the previous owner. If there are any outstanding debts, you should instruct your solicitor, or conveyancer, to make an agreement with the leaseholder and management company, which states that you are not liable for these debts. This must be done before the exchange of contracts.

Leasehold properties can have a number of restrictions on what you can do within the property. The HIP should contain information about these restrictions, the terms of the lease and the amount of ground rent that is payable, but if you are unclear, you should ask further questions of the selling agent. Also, you should note that properties which have a short lease left on them tend to be harder to sell, so you will need to take this into account when you decide to dispose of the property in the future. More information about leasehold can be obtained from the Leasehold Advisory Service (www.lease-advice.org).

Commonhold

This is a newer form of land ownership that relates to blocks of flats and other buildings that are made up of individual units. Under commonhold, a block of flats is owned jointly by all the owners of the flats and, unlike leasehold, there is no overall landlord. In the building, each unit is held as freehold and the common parts of the building are held and managed by a commonhold association. This is a private limited company of which the unit holders are members. The commonhold association is responsible for maintaining the common areas of the building and all the members must sign a statement, called a commonhold agreement, in which they agree to keep to certain terms and conditions.

This type of ownership has implications for the type of development you are able to undertake and on what else you are able to do in your flat, so you need to ask further questions before making purchasing decisions. A disadvantage of commonhold is that the members of the commonhold association must enforce the rules in the commonhold agreement, which may cause tension between neighbours. An advantage to this type of ownership is that you do not have to rely on absent landlords to manage and maintain your building, and you have more control on how the building is managed.

If the repossessed flat in which you are interested is commonhold, you should check that the commonhold association is properly registered as a company limited by guarantee at Companies House (www.companies house.gov.uk), as this will help to safeguard your investment. If it has been registered for some time, you will be able to confirm the financial health of the association and view its previous filed accounts. Also, it is important to check the Commonhold Community Statement as this will provide details of how the building is managed and what rules are in place relating to the use and occupation of the units and the common parts.

Your solicitor, or conveyancer, should check that all of the paperwork and registration documents are in order and if there are any problems, you will be alerted to these. If any problems are serious, such as the commonhold association has not been registered properly, your solicitor may advise that you pull out of the sale.

When you are buying a commonhold property that has been repossessed, you must make sure that all of the required funds have been paid to the association. This is because, as the new owner, you could be liable for debts, such as missed service charge payments, left by the previous owner.

Conveyancing in Scotland

In Scotland, the conveyancing process begins before bids are made on a property and concludes once a binding contract has been made between solicitors acting for the buyer and seller. This is called 'concluding Missives' and will only be done when all conditions have been met and accepted by your solicitor and when all paperwork has been checked and is in order. This includes checks on the legal ownership of the property and local searches (see page 138). Your solicitor will then prepare the relevant documents, including what is known as a 'disposition', which transfers ownership of the property to you. The Missives (or contract) will specify a date of entry to the property. This is known as 'completion' and is the date by which all monies have to be paid and the keys to the property are passed to you.

PROBLEMS ASSOCIATED WITH REPOSSESSIONS

When you buy a property that has been repossessed, you are buying from the lender rather than an individual seller. A lender is able to stress that it has not lived at the property and is therefore unable to provide specific information about the property that would normally be supplied by someone who had lived in the house. Therefore, you need to take extra care when you are viewing a repossessed property, so that you can pick up on any potential problems with the structure, fittings and fixtures. Also, you need to make sure that you commission a detailed survey and you view the property again between making an offer and the exchange of contracts. This will ensure that there has not been any additional damage caused by previous owners accessing the property, once they have been evicted. More information about viewing a property and commissioning a survey is provided in Chapter 7.

'The buyer is free to view the property before the exchange of contracts takes place and is encouraged to do so. Estate agents/lenders are responsible for the keys. Any redress for damage should always be agreed before the exchange of contracts takes place. Insurance must always be put in place from the date of the exchange of contracts, and not completion.'

A P Malam Property Lawyers, Conwy.

You should also note that, in many cases, a list of fittings and fixtures will not be included for a property that has been repossessed, as the lender will not state what is to be included in the sale (see the extract from the report of contract below). It is important that you view the property on several occasions before the exchange of contracts, so that you know what will be included in the sale and so you can make sure that this does not change during the conveyancing process.

When you are buying a repossessed property, many lenders who are selling will insist that there is a simultaneous exchange of contracts and completion. (Exchange of contracts occurs when identical copies of the contracts are signed and exchanged by the seller and buyer. This is the moment when the transaction becomes legally binding. Completion is the date by which you make full payment and the property is now yours.) Indeed, you may find that your solicitor, or conveyancer, also aims for this simultaneous exchange and completion as it avoids any problems regarding damage to the property between exchange and completion, it reduces the risk of the buyer pulling out, and it enables the lender to recoup its money quicker than it would normally do so.

'Worth a mention is that all the repossessions I have dealt with have actually had a simultaneous exchange and completion – this avoids the risk of any damage between the exchange and completion and, of course, prevents distressed clients and unhappy buyers. Failing a simultaneous exchange and

completion, which I always try to aim for, I will warn clients as much as possible of the dangers of squatters, damage before exchange, etc., but the only ideal solution would be to actually have the client sitting in the property itself as we exchange contracts!'

A P Malam Property Lawyers, Conwy.

EXTRACT FROM REPORT OF CONTRACT

Re: Your Proposed Purchase of [*property's address*].

We have now received the main part of the Contract paperwork for [*property's address*] and, having read through the Contract documentation provided by the Seller's Solicitor, we would point out the following to you and would ask you to read through all the information provided very carefully before you proceed with your purchase.

Please note that if you do not have a survey or inspection carried out and you do not find out about any problems with the property until after exchange of Contracts, it is too late to do anything about it. Any expenses incurred, as a result thereof, are your sole responsibility. This is known as the doctrine of 'caveat emptor', which means 'let the buyer beware'. This applies in particular to your situation, as the property you are buying is a repossession and so is currently unoccupied. It is extremely important that you view the property again before the exchange of Contracts to ensure that the property has remained as viewed when you made your offer to purchase.

TITLE of the property you are purchasing

The property is freehold and is registered under Title Number [*title number*] and the title is absolute title, which is the best form of title the Land Registry can give to land.

A copy of the plan to the property is attached. You will note that the plan shows red outlining and you will own the whole of the property within this red outline. The plan is not intended to show the precise location of each boundary; these should be checked on site and any significant discrepancies referred to us, so that we can seek clarification from the Seller. Please note that the plan provided is the plan which has been provided to us by the Seller's Solicitor. If you are of the opinion that the plan does not include the whole of the property you intend to purchase, or you are aware that the Seller owns additional surrounding land which should be included in the sale to you, please inform us immediately and we shall make further enquiries.

You should inspect the property to ensure that it is not currently occupied or appears to be occupied and let us know if this is not the case. The property is being sold to you with full vacant possession on completion.

Rights granted to you

[*Details*]

Restrictive covenants (Those things which you cannot do at the property)

[*Details*]

Agreement

You will agree to [*details*].

INFORMATION FROM THE SELLER

A package of information completed by the Seller is normally enclosed as follows:

1. **Seller's Property Information Form.** This provides information on boundaries, disputes, notices, guarantees, services, rights and other services, if any.

    If you have not already done so, we would strongly urge you to check all appliances and services at the property and, in particular, ask the Seller to demonstrate to you the central heating system so that you understand how the system functions and so you can also check that it is in full working order.

2. **List of Fixtures, Fittings and Contents Questionnaire.** This indicates which items at the property are included in the sale and which are not.

The above forms are not provided where the Seller is a mortgagee in possession. It is, therefore, extremely important that you view the property prior to the exchange of Contracts – none of the fixtures and fittings will be included in the sale price.

THE PURCHASE CONTRACT

The Contract is in the form incorporating the Standard Conditions of Sale, which are widely used for residential transactions. The main provisions of the Contract are as follows:

1. The purchase price is £[*property's price*].

2. On exchange of Contracts you will pay a deposit of ten per cent (or other by agreement). If we cannot complete the purchase of your property due to the Seller's default, you will become entitled to the return of the deposit (and you may be able to claim damages for any loss suffered). However, this also applies should you, as the Buyer, default and you may forfeit the deposit paid and be liable for damages for loss suffered.

    Furthermore, the Seller may also seek a remedy of 'specific performance', which, in simple terms, means that the Seller can seek an order that you proceed with the Contract and purchase of the property. Remedies for breach of Contract, on the other hand, are also available to you should the Seller default and refuse to proceed with the Contract.

3. The pre-agreed completion date will be inserted on the exchange of Contracts. This date will be the date on which the transaction is to be completed and the Seller must vacate the property on that date. We must send the completion monies to the Seller's Solicitor to reach the Solicitor's bank account by 2pm that day. You will be liable to pay daily interest at four per cent above the bank base rate if cleared funds are not made available to us in time to remit the completion monies early enough, so we will need to receive the funds (other than the loan from your Building Society) from you either by Banker's draft or by telegraphic transfer into this firm's account, preferably on the day before the completion date. Nearer the time we will let you know how much is required; this will include a sum to cover fees,

disbursements paid or payable (including Stamp Duty Land Tax and registration fees).

4. You are buying the property in its actual state and condition. You must be satisfied about this from your own inspection of the property and from your Surveyor's report. If you expect the Seller to remedy (or pay for the remedy of) any defects, this will have to be agreed with the Seller before Contracts are exchanged and special provisions must be added to the Contract.

5. Once Contracts are exchanged, you should arrange for your insurance on the property to take effect from this date. We will require a copy of the insurance schedule prior to exchange of Contracts so that we can ensure that the insurance meets with your Lender's requirements. We shall be unable to exchange without this.

A P Malam Property Lawyers, Conwy.

SUMMARY

The conveyancing process is the legal procedure involved in transferring buildings and/or land from one owner to another and dealing with the financial transactions. This includes the preparation and exchange of contracts, searches, investigation of title and checking that the financial arrangements are in place. When you are buying a repossession, fixtures and fittings will not be included in the sale price. The lender, who is selling, has not lived in the property and, therefore, has 'no knowledge' of conditions, disputes, damage and other problems that may be present.

Once the conveyancing process has been completed successfully and you have exchanged contracts and completed on the property, you can move into your new home. But there are certain issues which you should be aware of when you are moving into a property which has been repossessed. These issues are discussed in the following chapter.

CHAPTER 11:

MOVING INTO A REPOSSESSED PROPERTY

 *'It went surprisingly well really, all things considered. I think the whole process took about nine weeks, quicker than I expected. I know they wanted to make a quick sale so that made it easier and us not being part of a chain helped. So we moved in really quickly, but it did take us a long time to get the place in some sort of order. It did really, but now, as you can see, it's lovely. We're so happy here.'*

Kate, Dorset.

Once you have been successful in acquiring your repossessed property, you need to make sure that it is in a safe and suitable condition before you move in. For some people, this is a smooth and quick process, as Kate illustrates in the quotation above. But, for other people, the process is much more time-consuming, and involves a careful assessment of personal risk and property safety, as outlined in Case Study 6 below. Also, when you move into a property that has been repossessed, you need to make sure that you inform all of the relevant organisations and that you reconnect all the services, if they have been disconnected. Information about these issues is provided in this chapter.

ASSESSING RISK AND SAFETY

Case Study 6 below paints a graphic picture of the dangerous condition in which some repossessed properties can be left when previous owners have been evicted. It is important that you carry out a thorough inspection to assess risk and safety, prior to your moving in or turning on the services. While it is the responsibility of the lender to make sure that the house is in a safe condition, my research has shown that this clearly does not always happen, as described below.

CASE STUDY 6: JOHN

The following email was received from John, a retired building services engineer and the father of someone who had bought a repossessed property. It has been reproduced in its entirety as it provides a graphic example of the problems that can be encountered when you are moving into a house that has been repossessed.

'Dear Catherine.

When my son and his wife bought their first house in 1998, they were informed that it had been repossessed by the building society and was, therefore, competitively priced. They were also advised to get professional advice before they moved in as to the state of the utilities.

I am a retired building services engineer and, at that time, one of my work colleagues, who had previously worked as an electrician for a local council/housing association, gave me lots of advice as he had experience of making safe houses from which tenants had been evicted.

On the day my son and daughter-in-law picked up the keys I told them not to turn on any of the services until I had done a thorough inspection. There was no structural damage, just a level of vandalism to the utilities. All power was off and all water services had been isolated and drained, including the central heating.

The defects found were as follows:

- *The power supply cable to the electric shower was disconnected and pulled up into the loft. The bare conductors on this cable were so placed as to make contact with the head of any unsuspecting person entering the unlit loft.*

- *The control box for the shower had been ripped from the bathroom wall.*

- *Several electric cables running through the loft space had been randomly cut, with bare conductors left exposed.*

- *The plastic ball had been removed from the arm of the float valve in both toilet cisterns.*

- *The seal between the toilet pedestal and waste pipe had been removed.*

- *The connection between the thermostatic valve and the radiator had been slackened off in many cases, thus creating a potential leak.*

These problems were all identified and rectified fairly quickly and we were able to put on the power and water and have a cup of tea.

However, there was one defect that did not manifest itself until a couple of weeks later when it was discovered that the airing cupboard was getting wet. After removing the insulation jacket, a small pinhole was found in the hot water cylinder. A panel pin had been carefully inserted into the side of the cylinder so that it had a degree of self-sealing. As this steel panel pin corroded, it caused the cylinder to leak, which was quite difficult to detect but easy to fix with a blob of solder.

My work colleague had advised me not to walk on any stair tread or floor that was carpeted before testing the weight-bearing properties, as it was not unusual to have floorboards removed beneath the carpet or for newel posts to be partly sawn through. None of these were discovered, so I think we got off rather lightly.

You really have to appreciate, if not admire, the ingenuity of some of these folks in what must be a very stressful time. This was not a house in a deprived low income area, but a detached house in a fairly affluent area of Woking in Surrey.

Hope this is of use to you. You may use it however you wish.

Regards, John.'

Sold as seen

A repossessed property will be stated to be 'sold as seen'. Also, because of the legal doctrine of 'caveat emptor' ('let the buyer beware'), the onus is on you to make sure that everything is in working order and safe. Although the seller must not deliberately mislead the buyer, it is the buyer who must make sure that the property is in a condition that he wants. With a property that has been repossessed, a lender will state that it has no knowledge about the condition of appliances, fixtures and fittings. It is, therefore, very important that you check that all of the appliances, central heating and other systems are in good working order before you commit to the exchange of contracts (if they have not been removed from the property). If you are in doubt, you should employ fully qualified professionals, such as electricians or plumbers, to inspect the services and installations for you (see below).

If you do find any damage or deliberate sabotage, you can negotiate a reduction in the selling price or request that the problems are rectified before the exchange of contracts. If they are not rectified satisfactorily, or the lender will not reduce the selling price, it is your prerogative to pull out of the sale.

Undertaking a safety inspection

Case Study 6 illustrates that repossessed properties can be placed on the market in a serious and dangerous condition. Some of the problems outlined above would not have been spotted unless a detailed inspection had been carried out by an expert. If you do not have the necessary knowledge and skills to detect such problems, it is important that you ask an expert to assess the condition of the property before you move in. This is in addition to the survey that you will have already commissioned on the property. Although this will have highlighted structural problems, and other problems with the condition of the property, surveyors cannot remove fixtures and fittings or enter areas that are difficult to access. Therefore, you will need to ask someone else to undertake this task once you have purchased the property.

Depending on the type of property and the condition in which it has been left, there are a variety of professionals you can call in to undertake a safety inspection, as discussed below.

Electrical safety inspections

If you have bought a property that has been repossessed (or indeed any property), you have no idea when the electrics were last inspected, if at all, and you have no idea who installed or worked on the installations prior to your ownership. Also, as we have seen in Case Study 6, angry previous owners can leave the electrics in a dangerous state for the next occupant.

The Electrical Safety Council (ESC) points out that, each year, there are around 21 fatal and 2,788 non-fatal electric shock accidents in the home (www.electricalsafetycouncil.org.uk). Also, 7,909 fires are caused by electrical faults, which result in 15 deaths and 1,100 injuries each year. In an attempt to cut down on these injuries and fatalities, the government has introduced new electrical safety laws. These state that anyone carrying out work on, or installing, fixed electrical installations in households in England, Wales and Scotland must be an approved electrical contractor. More information on these standards can be obtained from the National Inspection Council for Electrical Installation Contracting (NICEIC) (www.niceic.org.uk) or, if you live in Scotland, from the Scottish Buildings Standards Agency (SBSA) (www.sbsa.gov.uk).

Electrical installations must be designed and installed in a way that provides protection against mechanical and thermal damage, and so that they do not present electric shock and fire hazards to people. All installations must be suitably inspected and tested to verify that they meet the relevant equipment and installation standards. It is recommended that an electrical inspection of the home should take place every ten years, yet a survey conducted by the ESC found that 48 per cent of those surveyed did not realise that this should happen. As the owner of a new property, and especially one that has been repossessed, you should commission an inspection by a fully qualified and registered electrician. You can find an electrician by visiting www.competentperson.co.uk, or by using the online database of the NICEIC.

Types of inspection

Most companies will offer two types of inspection – a routine electrical inspection or a periodic inspection. If you are in any doubt about the standard and condition of the electrics, you should obtain a periodic inspection, as it is much more detailed than a routine inspection. Prices vary, depending on the contractor that you use and the size, type and location of the property. In general, you can expect to pay £50–£100 for a routine inspection and £100–£250 for a periodic inspection.

Periodic inspection

The periodic inspection will check on the condition of an existing electrical installation, and identify any deficiencies against the national safety standard for electrical installations. In particular, the electrician will do the following during the inspection:

- Check to see whether the electrical circuits or equipment are overloaded.

- Identify any potential shock risks or fire hazards.

- Point out the adequacy of earthing and bonding.

- Point out any deliberate damage or sabotage.

- Highlight any defective DIY work.

- Assess wear and tear and deterioration.

- Point out where equipment may need replacing.

- Test wiring and associated fixed electrical equipment to check that it is safe.

The report will describe the overall condition of the electrical installation as either 'satisfactory', in which case no immediate remedial work is required, or 'unsatisfactory', which means that remedial work is required to make the installation safe to use. If the report highlights work that is needed to make the installation safe, you do not have to use the electrician that carried out the inspection. Instead, you should obtain quotations from at least three different electricians, making sure that they are approved contractors. Where the work required is considerable, you may find that you are unable to move into your new property until the work has been completed.

 This house is located in Northampton and was bought as a repossession by property investors in 1996 for £18,000. They are not sure how much below market value this property was, but they knew that it was a 'very good bargain'. When they acquired the house, the whole property was in need of complete modernisation and there was no inside bathroom, only an outside toilet and a tin bath located in the cellar. The property was extended to include a double cellar for an extra kitchen and a lounge, two new bathrooms were installed and the outside toilet was knocked down and replaced with another bedroom. In this way a three-bedroom terraced property was extended to a six-bedroom property that is let to students. The investors believe that they spent a further £70,000 on extending and making the property habitable, but they believe that it is now worth around £180,000.

Portable appliance inspection

The Health and Safety Executive (HSE) states that 25 per cent of all reported electrical accidents involve portable appliances. The National Association of Professional Inspectors and Testers (NAPIT) (www.napit. org.uk) defines a portable appliance as 'any electrical item which can, or is intended to be, moved while it is connected to an electrical supply'. This can include appliances such as air conditioning units, refrigerators, freezers, bathroom heaters and electric cookers. If any of these appliances have been left in the property, you should ask for an electrician to test them for safety, prior to use.

The cost of portable appliance testing varies, depending on the electrician that you use and the number of appliances that need testing, but it should be in the range of £50–£100 for up to ten appliances. You can find an approved contractor to inspect your appliances from NICEIC, ESC or NAPIT.

Gas safety inspection

Before you move into the property, you should ask a registered contractor to check all of the gas installations and appliances, again for the safety of you and your family. All inspections, installations and remedial work must be undertaken by an installer who is registered with the Council for Registered Gas Installers (CORGI), and who must have the correct qualifications to undertake the type of work you require. You can find a registered installer by contacting CORGI or using the online database (www.trustcorgi.com). Always ask to see the installer's CORGI identity card before you invite him into your property. He will check all of the gas installations and appliances, making sure that there is no damage left by the previous owners. In particular, the inspection will include the following checks, if they are relevant to the property you have purchased:

- A boiler inspection, which includes:
    - the suitability of position;
    - a flue test with a recording of the carbon monoxide level;
    - the suitability of ventilation;
    - the suitability of earthing;
    - the standard of pipework;
    - a check for performance;
    - a check for safety; and
    - a check for efficiency;
- A gas hob inspection, which includes:
    - a check of the isolation control;
    - a check of the ignition; and
    - a check that all of the burners are running correctly and are not blocked;
- A gas fire inspection, which includes:
    - a check of the fire and back plate;
    - a check of the chimney;
    - a test for spillage;
    - a check for performance;

- a check for efficiency; and

- an inspection for the correct ventilation.

The cost of gas safety inspections depends on the type of inspection required and the type and number of appliances in the property, but it should be in the region of £55–£100. Some companies will offer a discount on both gas and electrical inspections if you order both from the same company, but you must check that the company is approved to carry out both types of inspection. You can choose to have the boiler serviced at the same time that the inspection is carried out, and some companies will offer a discount if you decide on this course of action. This may be prudent as you have no idea when the boiler was last serviced. If the previous owner was struggling financially, having his boiler serviced may not have been a priority.

'Every time we put the boiler on it was really stinky. We thought that we'd better get it checked out. Apparently, it needed a really good clean and the water pressure was right down. I'm so glad we got it done because it could have been really dangerous.'

Female interviewee, who wishes to remain anonymous, south of England.

Inspections for landlords

If you are buying a repossessed property to let to tenants, you should note that the Landlord and Tenant Act 1995 requires landlords of properties with short leases to keep the electrical installations in good repair and proper working order. In addition to the first inspection that you will need to arrange when you purchase the property, the ESC recommends that landlords arrange for a periodic inspection to be carried out for tenanted properties at each change of occupancy. You will need to keep a copy of the report to give to tenants, if requested. Again, if remedial work is required, or if you need to install new appliances, it's advisable to obtain quotations from at least three different registered contractors so that you can get the best deal.

Portable appliance inspection

As a landlord, you are required to comply with the Portable Appliance Safety section of the Consumer Protection Act 1987 to ensure that all electrical items are safe. If any have been left in the property by the previous owner, these must be checked before you let the property. In addition to this, all portable electrical appliances must be inspected and tested regularly by a NICEIC-approved electrician. The Consumer Protection Act makes it an offence for a landlord to provide any portable electrical appliance which is either electrically or physically unsafe and which would be a danger to tenants or visitors to the property. More information can be obtained from the NICEIC website (www.niceic. org.uk).

Gas safety inspection

If you are intending to let the property to tenants, you should note that the Gas Safety (Installation and Use) Regulations 1998 state that all let and managed property must be tested when you first let the property, and then annually for safety. This must be done by a CORGI-registered installer. You should request a Landlord's Gas Safety Certificate after each inspection, a copy of which should be given to your tenants. Failure to comply with these regulations can result in a substantial fine or even imprisonment.

KNOWING WHO TO INFORM

When you move into a property that has been repossessed, there are various organisations that you should inform as this should help to reduce problems that you could face in the future. These are discussed below.

Utility companies

Take meter readings, including gas, electricity and water (if relevant) as soon as you complete on the property. This is the date when all the contracts have been signed and exchanged, all monies have been paid and the keys are passed to you. This will protect you against claims for fuel that you have not used (see Author's Note, below).

Finding out about the supplier

Once you have done this, you need to find out which utility companies were used by the previous occupants. In some cases, outstanding bills will have arrived through the post and the envelopes may contain details of the utility company, but you should note that it is illegal to open post that has been addressed to someone else (see page 162). Therefore, if the identity of the company is not clear from the envelope, you can find out who the electricity supplier is by calling your local distribution company. Each one keeps a record of who supplies electricity to every home in its area. When you contact the supplier, you need to speak to its Meter Point Administration Service (MPAS) and inform it of your address, including your postcode. Telephone numbers for the distribution companies are available on the Energywatch website (www.energywatch.org.uk). For gas suppliers, call Transco's Meter Helpline on 0870 608 1524 and ask it for the name of your registered supplier.

 **AUTHOR'S NOTE**

My research has shown that gas and electricity has been used between an offer being made and the completion date. In some cases, this has been a considerable amount and has led the new owners to believe that the evicted borrowers had been accessing the property while the sale was going through. You need to make sure that you only pay for fuel that is used once you have become the owner of the property. You only become liable once you have completed on the property, so make sure that you take a meter reading on that date and you do not pay for any fuel you have not used. Also, if you suspect that the evicted borrowers have been accessing the property, you should inform the estate agent and you should arrange for all of the locks to be changed immediately.

Once you have found out which utility companies have been used by the previous occupants, send each company a letter with the exact date that you moved into the property and your meter readings for that date. Make it clear that you are the new owner and that you have no idea of the whereabouts of the previous occupants. Include contact details of the lender that repossessed the property (if you are able to obtain these) and ask that all correspondence relating to the previous owners is addressed to them. If you cannot obtain details of the lender, provide contact details of the selling agent instead. Keep a copy of the letter so that you can refer to it if problems should arise at a later date.

'It was obvious – the electricity and gas bills kept coming in separate envelopes, but they were both embossed with EDF Energy, in re-usable envelopes that also contained their address. We just got in touch with them and then changed our supplier.'

Email from someone who wishes to remain anonymous, Plymouth.

Updating records

Unfortunately, some utility companies take a long time to update their records and you may find that you receive several demands for previous bills. But you cannot open post that is not addressed to you, as Postwatch illustrate in the following quotation:

'Postwatch appreciate that receiving post intended for individuals no longer living at an address can be irritating. Under the Postal Services Act 2000, a person commits an offence if he opens an item of post which he knows, or reasonably suspects, has been correctly delivered to the address – but addressed to a previous occupant. Royal Mail are obliged to deliver the post as addressed and advise that the only way to stop a mailing is at source. Score through the address with a pen and write on the front of the envelope NOT KNOWN AT THIS ADDRESS RETURN TO SENDER. Put the mail back into a post box – free of charge. If there is no return address visible, Royal Mail have a returned letter centre in Belfast where it is allowed to open the mail and repatriate with the

> *sender. The relevant database should then be amended and the mailings stop. If no suitable recipient can be established, the item will be destroyed.'*

Postwatch website, December 2007 (www.postwatch.co.uk).

Although you cannot open post addressed to a previous occupant, you should not ignore these demands. Return the envelopes in the manner described above and write again to the utility company explaining the situation. Again, keep all records of correspondence. In some cases, you may find it more successful to speak to the complaints department. If you are unable to resolve the issue, contact Energywatch and it will be able to act on your behalf to sort out the problems. Alternatively, you can contact the Energy Ombudsman, who will be able to decide what action should be taken (www.energy-ombudsman.org.uk).

Your local authority

When you move into your property, you need to contact your local authority so that when it next updates the electoral register, your details will be included. These updated registers are sent to credit reference agencies and once your details have been included, you should not have any problems with your credit rating at your new address. More information about credit reference agencies and your credit rating is provided in Chapter 12.

You can obtain a registration form from your local authority or download a form from its website. A separate entry needs to be made by each member of the household who is eligible to vote. Once you have completed the registration form, it should be returned to the Electoral Registration Office at the address printed on the form. It will then make the required changes and send the updated register to the credit reference agencies.

Council Tax

You should also inform the local authority that you have moved in for

Council Tax purposes. Again, specify the exact date that you moved in and make it clear that you do not know the whereabouts of the previous occupants, and instead include the contact details of the lender that repossessed the property, or the selling agent, if these details are not available. People who have been repossessed may have outstanding Council Tax debts, so you need to make it clear from the outset that these debts are nothing to do with you, as the new owner.

Council Tax is charged on a daily basis and the charge will begin on the day that you move in or complete on the property. If you have purchased a property that requires a considerable amount of work to make it habitable, and you leave it unoccupied and unfurnished, you may not have to pay Council Tax, as the property will be exempt for up to six months while it remains in that state. But you do need to check that the property has not been empty for a six-month period prior to your ownership as the exemption will have already been exhausted. Contact your local authority for more information.

TV licensing

Your TV licence does not automatically move with you when you move house. Therefore, you will need to notify TV Licensing as soon as you move into your new home, so that it can update your details to make sure that you are correctly licensed at your new address. It is important to do this as soon as you move into a repossessed property, as the previous occupants may not have paid their bill and this will be registered on the TV Licensing database. You can change your address quickly and easily by visiting its website. You will need to have your current TV licence number available to complete the form (www.tvlicensing.co.uk).

RECONNECTING SERVICES

In some cases, the gas or electricity may have been disconnected, especially if the previous occupants were unable to pay their bills. As long as the pipes are not damaged and if you can supply proof of your last address and show that you have a good track payment at your previous address, it should be no problem to get the services reconnected. But there may be a charge for this service. You can change your supplier at any time by giving 28 days' notice to the present supplier. If you choose to do this, both the old and new supplier will need informing and both will need an accurate meter reading for the day when the supplier changes over.

Repairing pipes

In cases where pipes have been left in a dangerous condition, they will need to be repaired before your supply can be reconnected. If the pipes are inside the house and its boundaries, they are your responsibility and you will have to pay for repairs. If they fall outside the house and boundaries as part of the mains, repairs and costs are the responsibility of the supplier. But in cases where pipes have been deliberately damaged and they are outside the property boundaries, utility companies may refuse to bear the cost, so you may have to seek legal advice specific to your circumstances.

In certain properties the pipes may be shared between neighbours and, in most cases, all of the neighbours should share the cost if the pipes are within their property boundaries. If the pipes have been deliberately damaged, you will need to use your discretion about whether you ask your neighbours to share the cost or if you pay for the work yourself to maintain goodwill (see quotation below).

'Although we shared the supply with our neighbours, we decided to pay for it ourselves. It wasn't too expensive and we thought it would help us to get on better with the neighbours. We told them about it and they offered to pay their share, but we turned them down. We get on well with them now!'

Email from someone who wishes to remain anonymous, Plymouth.

Prepayment meters

In houses where a prepayment meter has been installed, you must transfer the supply into your name. If you use the previous occupant's card or key, any money you pay will be credited to his account. If you have a good previous record with your utility supply company, you can contact the company to find out about changing the prepayment meter. You should do this as soon as you can, as this type of payment system tends to be more expensive than other options.

SUMMARY

When you move into a property that has been repossessed it is important to assess risk and safety, especially when the previous occupants have caused damage or if the property is in a state of disrepair. It is important to obtain the relevant gas and safety checks before you switch on the supply as this will protect you and your family against unsafe or deliberately damaged installations. Once you have moved into the property, there are various organisations that you should inform, as this should help to reduce any problems that you could face in the future. These include utility supply companies, your local authority and TV Licensing.

Living in a repossessed property may pose other problems that may not be immediately apparent, but which can manifest themselves at a later date, such as visits or letters from debt collectors or problems with your credit rating. These issues are discussed in the following chapter.

CHAPTER 12:

LIVING IN A REPOSSESSED PROPERTY

'Everything went quite well, all things considered. It took us so long to sell our house I really thought that [the lender] would pull out, but it hung on for us. So I think it took about five months all in all. But when we moved in it was all fine until our neighbour told us that he'd got a letter asking us if we knew who lived in our house. He showed me the letter and it really was quite aggressive, almost threatening. Trouble is that there was no address on it, just a telephone number, premium rate. I wasn't going to pay to find out who it was from. Then we started getting visits from burly men. It was quite intimidating and it took us a long time to stop it all. But, fingers crossed, we haven't had a visit for over three years now.'

Janet, by email, south of England.

The quotation from Janet above illustrates that you can encounter problems once you have moved into a property that has been repossessed, although these problems may become apparent only after you have lived in the property for some time. If you are intending to buy a property that has been repossessed, it is important to gain an awareness of the types of problems that can occur and that you understand your rights, so that you know how to deal with any problems if they arise.

The types of problems that you may encounter could be due to inaccurate or out-of-date information that is held by credit reference agencies or problems from people and organisations that are chasing the debts left by the previous occupants. These issues are discussed in this chapter.

CHECKING AND CHANGING DETAILS HELD BY A CREDIT REFERENCE AGENCY

Although your credit rating should not be based on the property, if you apply for credit before the records have been changed on your new property, you may experience problems obtaining credit. This is because the lender uses the electoral register, held by the credit reference agencies, to confirm that the client lives at that address. If your name does not appear on the register at that property, you may be refused credit. This problem can be rectified in three main ways:

1. By informing the local authority as soon as you move in.

2. By asking the organisation that you want to borrow money from to check the electoral register at your previous address. You may need to provide proof of the date you moved house and you may have to explain that the house you have moved into was repossessed.

3. By providing several types of evidence to show that you live at your current address.

Obtaining your credit report

If your new details have been included on the electoral register, but you still find that you are experiencing problems obtaining credit, you can ascertain the nature of the problem by obtaining a credit report from one of the three credit reference agencies (contact details can be found in Appendix 2: Useful Organisations). There will be a charge for a full report, although, at the time of writing this book, two of the three companies are offering a free 30-day trial.

A credit report can include the following information:

- Your name, address and date of birth.

- Your social security number.

- Your previous addresses.

- Your current and previous employers.

- Public records, such as bankruptcies or court judgments.

- Previous credit searches and who has been looking.

- Your credit card, mortgage and loan payment history.

- Your credit score and what it means.

Knowing who can access your credit report

Lenders and service providers use your credit report to make decisions about whether or not you may be a credit risk. It helps them to decide whether they are going to lend you money and if so, how much interest they will charge. People who are able to look at your credit report with a 'permissible purpose', as defined by law, include the following:

- Potential lenders.

- Insurance companies.

- Government agencies, although they may be allowed to view only certain portions.

- Landlords, if they have your written consent.

- Employers and potential employers, if they have your written consent.

- Companies that you allow to monitor your account for signs of identity theft.

- Someone who uses your credit report to provide a product or service you have requested.

- Someone who has your written authorisation to obtain your credit report. It is a criminal offence to obtain someone else's credit report, unless you have written authorisation to do so.

No one can search your records without your permission. Your permission is usually obtained when you sign a loan application form or tick a consent form (whether paper or online). Therefore, all of the small print should be read carefully, so that you know when you are giving permission for your records to be searched. Companies arranging finance by telephone should make it clear, verbally, that a credit search will be carried out.

 This property is also located in Northampton and was bought as a repossession in 2005 for almost £130,000, which was about £10,000 below the average market value in that area. It was purchased by property investors who undertook a cellar and loft conversion, costing around £60,000. The property is now let to students and the investors believe it is now worth around £220,000. They see their investment as a long-term investment and, therefore, believe that they obtained a good bargain that will go up in value, despite short-term fluctuations in the market.

Rectifying inaccuracies and mistakes

If you check your credit report and you find that there are inaccuracies or mistakes, you can take action to rectify the problem. Initially, you should contact the appropriate creditor, or lender, as it has standard procedures for customers who have a complaint about its account. The situation should be resolved quickly if you are able to prove that a mistake has been made. You should keep records of all correspondence.

If the problem cannot be resolved with the lender, you will need to contact the credit reference agency direct. The agency will conduct an investigation and alter the mistakes if the investigation is successful. Although the other credit agencies should, eventually, alter their records, this can take some time, so you may find it quicker to contact each agency to get your records updated.

Unresolved problems

In cases where it is not possible for you to resolve a problem, you are able to add a short statement to your file, explaining the nature of your disagreement. This will be available to view when lenders access your file. More information about your credit report can be obtained from the credit reference agencies listed in Appendix 2: Useful Organisations.

'I had a feeling that something wasn't quite right because my partner and I had opened a joint bank account two weeks before, and we had got a mortgage with no trouble at all. But when we moved in, we wanted to get some things from Debenhams, but they refused us when we applied for a store card. We wanted the card because you could get ten per cent off everything and we needed a lot of things for the house. I had never been turned down for anything and my partner hadn't either. Eventually, someone told us it may be to do with the new address. We had recently filled in a form that came through the post about voting and, after that, we never had any trouble. It was a bit embarrassing, though, being turned down by Debenhams.'

Louise, Bournemouth.

DEALING WITH DEBT COLLECTORS

In some cases, and despite all your hard work informing the relevant people, debt collectors can hassle you when you move into a repossessed property, whether it is by telephone, letter or face-to-face. Creditors use debt collection agencies to chase debts, but you should note that they are not court officials and they do not have the same powers as bailiffs. They cannot enter your home, seize possessions, harass, intimidate or act in a threatening manner. If any debt collectors do this, you should report them immediately to the police or to your local authority's Trading Standards department.

It is important to note, also, that debt collectors cannot pursue third parties for payment when they are not liable. Therefore, it is important that you keep all of the records of your house purchase, and the date you moved in, as well as proof of your identity, so that you can prove that you are not the person owing the debt. But debt collectors should not demand this information and you are not obliged to provide it, unless you would like to do so because you feel that it will help your case. If a debt collector refuses to acknowledge that you are not the debtor and continues to pursue you for the previous occupant's debt, again, you should report him to Trading Standards.

Sending demands

When they are chasing debts, the collectors cannot send demands to an individual when it is not certain that the individual is the debtor in question. This means that they should not send letters to 'the occupier' at your address or ask to speak to 'the occupier' on the telephone. In addition to this, they should not disclose details of the debt to a third party; for example, by addressing a letter to 'the occupier' in which they say how much is owed. Again, any type of unfair practice such as this should be reported immediately.

Once you have informed a debt collector that you are not the debtor, he should cease all of his collection activities, although several people in my research have said that it often takes a while for these activities to stop.

'I know that you're not supposed to open other people's mail, but we got so fed up with them coming through the door that we opened one in the end. It was demanding £32. I couldn't believe they had been sending these letters for over three years for £32 and they had been ignoring us when we kept writing 'moved away' and 'not known at this address'. I wrote a long letter explaining when we had moved in, that the other owners had left and nobody knew where they had gone; that we had bought the house, and so on. We got about three more letters and then, eventually, they seemed to get the message and it stopped.'

Female interviewee, who wishes to remain anonymous, south of England.

KNOWING YOUR RIGHTS AND RESPONSIBILITIES

There are various Acts of Parliament that help to protect your rights as a consumer. An awareness of legislation will help you to understand your rights if you should encounter any problems when you buy a repossessed property.

The Data Protection Act

The Data Protection Act gives you the right to know what information is held about you, and it sets out rules to make sure that companies handle this information in the correct manner. Companies have to comply with eight important principles, which state that data must be as follows:

1. Fairly and lawfully processed.

2. Processed for limited purposes.

3. Adequate, relevant and not excessive.

4. Accurate and up to date.

5. Not kept for longer than is necessary.

6. Processed in line with your rights.

7. Secure.

8. Not transferred to other countries without adequate protection.

If you have a complaint about the way that your personal data is held, you can ask the Information Commissioner's Office (ICO) to intervene. For example, you may access your credit history file because you have encountered some problems obtaining credit since you purchased your repossession and you find that the information being held is inaccurate. Under the fourth principle of the Data Protection Act outlined above, information must be accurate and up to date, so you should contact the credit reference agency to get the information changed. If the agency does not update your information to your satisfaction, you can contact the ICO (www.ico.gov.uk) as it has legal powers to ensure that organisations comply with the requirements of the Data Protection Act.

Another part of the Act states that individuals have the right to find out what personal information is held on computer and included in most paper records. This is useful if you find that you are being refused credit, for example, and you need to access records that are being held about you. When you request personal records, there may be a charge for this service. If you feel that you are being denied access to your personal records, you can apply to the ICO for help. Although most complaints are dealt with informally, it is possible for the ICO to take enforcement action if problems are not resolved.

The Freedom of Information Act

If you want to find out information that is held by public authorities, which does not relate to your personal data, you can make a request under the Freedom of Information Act. This may be useful if you wish to find out about the local authority's policy on debt collection agencies, for example. Most requests are free, although you may be asked to pay for photocopying costs.

This Act enables you to request information from any public authority and it must supply this information within 20 working days. If you want to make a request under this Act, you must do so in writing, which can be by letter, email or fax. You need to state your name and address and clearly describe the information you are requesting. Public authorities will not provide any information that breaches the Data Protection Act, or if its release would prejudice national security or damage commercial interests. More information about the Data Protection Act and the Freedom of Information Act can be obtained from the ICO.

The Consumers, Estate Agents and Redress Act 2007

This Act covers three policy areas. The first concerns the voice of the consumer, and brings together organisations, such as Energywatch and Postwatch, into a National Consumer Council to fight for the rights of the consumer. It also requires energy suppliers and postal service suppliers to belong to a redress scheme that enables complaints to be resolved and compensation to be awarded where warranted. This part of the Act should help you to seek redress if an energy supplier causes difficulties when you wish to reconnect, change or repair the supply in your new home.

The second part of the Act requires estate agents to join an approved redress scheme which will be used to handle complaints against estate agents made by people buying and selling residential property. It will allow enforcement action to be taken against agents who do not join the scheme, but who continue to operate as estate agents. Also, estate agents will be required to keep adequate records of their dealings with a client for six years. The Office of Fair Trading (OFT) will be able to inspect estate agents' files, when it is deemed necessary. This part of the Act will help you to seek redress against an estate agent who you believe has treated you unfairly (see Chapter 8 for more information about this part of the Act).

The third part of the Act covers doorstep selling, extending cancellation rights and cooling-off periods to solicited salespeople. This is useful if you change your mind about obtaining new windows or doors from a particular company that you contacted, for example. Previously the Act only covered unsolicited doorstep sales. More information about this Act can be obtained from the Department for Business, Enterprise and Regulatory Reform (BERR) (www.berr.gov.uk).

SUMMARY

If you decide to buy a property that has been repossessed, you need to be aware that some problems may arise at a later date, once you have moved into the property. This could include problems with debt collectors or difficulties with your credit rating. An understanding of your rights and responsibilities and an awareness of the types of problems that can occur will help you to deal with them, if they should occur, while you are living in the property. You can request personal information that is held about you under the Data Protection Act, and you can request general information held by public authorities under the Freedom of Information Act.

Buying properties that have been repossessed can provide you with the opportunity to obtain a home at a good price, often below market value. As the credit crunch begins to bite, the number of repossessions in the UK will continue to rise. While this is unfortunate for people who have lost their homes, it does provide an opportunity for others to obtain a property at a cheaper price than they may do otherwise. But there are a number of problems associated with buying repossessions. An awareness of these issues will help you to overcome these problems so that you can enjoy your new home or make the most of your investment property. Advice about all of these issues has been offered throughout this book. Some examples of properties that have been repossessed follow, along with some personal examples related via email. I hope you have enjoyed reading this book and find it useful. I wish you every success with your purchase.

APPENDIX 1:
PERSONAL EXAMPLES

As part of my research for this book, I sent a letter to local newspapers and newsletters across the south of England inviting people to email me with information about their personal experiences of buying repossessed property. Readers were very helpful, often providing long and detailed emails, and giving examples of what they would do differently, with the benefit of hindsight. Some of these emails are quoted throughout the book and some are reproduced below. The only changes that have been made are the removal of personal details, such as names and addresses, unless people have been happy for me to leave them as they are.

EMAIL 1: NIGEL AND KATRINA

'I noticed your article in the West Country Landlord's Association newsletter and I was interested to tell you of our experiences. We've been buying properties for our business for the last 15 years. We buy properties as cheap as we can, Nigel does them up and I let them to holidaymakers. It's a full time job for both of us. We live in an area where there are a lot of second homes and a lot of guest houses. Recently, we've noticed both of these types of places coming onto the market and being offered at our local auction. And quite a few of these are repossessions, although I think some people are selling them before they are being repossessed. We've been going to the auction since we started our business and I have to say that there are loads more of this type of property coming up now.

A couple of years ago the auction used to be really full with all sorts of people and it was hard to find much of a bargain. Now there are less people there and there seems to be a lot more bargains coming up. We're lucky, though, because we both work full time in the business and Nigel is very good at doing places up. So we look for the cheapest places we can find. At the moment, there are quite a lot about. I have a little niggle about making a profit from other people's misfortunes, but then, I guess, someone has to do it. Nigel has no problem though. He likes the bargains and he likes to get his teeth stuck into them.'

EMAIL 2: MRS PERCIVAL

'I read your letter in the *Dorset Echo* last Saturday. I bought my gorgeous little cottage at an auction two years ago. I won't go into detail about how much it cost, but I know that I was very lucky and got a gorgeous place very cheaply. Mind you, I would have been devastated if I hadn't got it because I fell in love with it the first time I saw it. I've been happy here ever since and I've had no problems. I don't know who lived in my cottage before me, but they must have been very sad to have to leave it in that way. I bought the cottage with cash, so I will never be repossessed.'

EMAIL 3: IAIN

'My wife and I bought the house…in May 1992. It was advertised in a local estate agents' window…with an asking price of £42,500. We initially viewed the property in January 1992 and completed towards the end of May 1992.

Before the sale/completion

The property had been repossessed and, as far as we could establish, it had been empty for around 18 months to two years (the previous owners had done a moonlight flit!).

The agent's description and the physical state of the property didn't quite match up, to say the least! With hindsight, we were probably quite naive when we were dealing with the estate agent, as we could, and should, have done more to drive a harder bargain and secure the sale at a much lower price. The agent was looking after his own interests, i.e. maximising his commission on the sale. The previous owners had mortgaged the property through a company, which I believe was connected with the estate agent's chain. Therefore, it was fair to assume that they would have been delighted that someone was showing an interest in their repossessed property, giving them the chance to recoup their money.

I assumed, at the time, that they would have been glad to move the property from their books (due to the length of time it had been vacant) by accepting a reasonable offer. We had a couple of offers turned down, which took us by surprise, and, although I will never be able to prove it, I strongly believe that the agent kept the sale price artificially high (i.e. he didn't fully consult with the mortgage company) so he could secure his commission.

The property was very run down with damage throughout, including a significant leak from the central heating system, which had caused the ceilings to collapse in several rooms. There was a pile of junk mail the size of a small mountain by the front door (a very nice feature!). It was evident that the mortgage company/estate agent failed to carry out any form of maintenance or made no effort to try and protect the property by, for example, draining down the central heating system or the water storage tanks. We had no documentation to support the serviceability of the boiler and we were not offered any reassurances from the agent either. We had a house buyer's survey carried out, which highlighted various faults which had to be rectified, before our lender would release all of the funds for the mortgage. We were able to negotiate with the estate agent for a reduction in the asking price and agreed a sale at £37,500, but we then spent between £5,500 and £6,000 on repair work, so effectively it cost us the asking price or more.

The garden was described as mature, but it was more like a jungle, with the grass over three feet high, and it was littered with all sorts of junk. It was a haven for discarded children's toys and other rubbish, which was all hidden within the 'jungle' grass, until a petrol-driven strimmer helped uncover all sorts. The grass also provided a wildlife haven for dozens of slow-worms! The agent's notes described the inclusion of a garden shed, which was a complete joke. It was totally dilapidated with no roof and it was in danger of total collapse. I recall, at the time, that it would have been more precise to describe it as a Baghdad garden shed (post the first Gulf War!).

After the sale

Within our junk mail feature were numerous final demand letters/bills for the previous occupants. Over several years we were also contacted by debt collection companies and bailiffs who were chasing debts belonging to the previous owners. We had concerns about the possibility that we were ending up on credit blacklists or were being pursued for debts which didn't belong to us.

As we settled into life within the community and got to know some of our neighbours and regulars at the local pub, people would often say to us, 'You live in Bob's house'. It was mildly amusing to start with, but it dragged on for quite a while until we reached a point where we had to make it clear 'that we didn't live in Bob's house! Bob had done a runner years' ago! This was our house!'

In conclusion

I think we would be more wary if we were to buy a repossessed property again, although, that said, we definitely learned a lot from our experiences in buying this house. Some of the lessons learned were quite harsh (e.g. never fully trust the estate agent and take much of what he says with a pinch of salt). I think that we paid more for the house than we should have done. With changes in the law governing how estate agents operate now, I'd like to think that most of them are now considered more reputable.

- I would definitely do more research about the property before committing to buying.

- I would try to ensure that 'my new address' was not connected with anyone else's debt or shortcomings.

- I would check the property's title deeds very carefully and, in particular, the layout of the property's boundaries, as I have a current boundary dispute with one of my neighbours (but it is not connected to the original purchase of the property).'

EMAIL 4: MR BETANT

'I am writing to you in response to your request for information about repossessed houses. My son bought a house several years ago that had been repossessed by the mortgage company. He certainly got the house very cheaply, and my wife and I were very impressed with his bargaining skills. My son was in business in the city and wanted a place in the country near us, so that when he came to visit he could stay in his own place. He also wanted somewhere as an investment. Apparently, he did it all over the World Wide Web. He didn't even visit an estate agent, but just asked them to send him information about properties that were coming onto the market. How times have changed.

They sent him details about this property and we visited it for him to see what it was like. It was in a bit of a state, but not too bad. It had huge potential and we told him so. He spoke to the estate agent who told him that it had been repossessed. We hadn't even found that out when we went to visit. But, as I say, my son is very good at negotiating. He didn't tell us how much he offered or how much the estate agent accepted, but knowing my son it would have been well below the asking price. All he says is that he got a real bargain. He has done the place up and it's very smart. He has done a good professional job on it.'

APPENDIX 2:
USEFUL ORGANISATIONS

ADVISORY BODY

Leasehold Advisory Service (LEASE)

LEASE provides free advice on the law affecting residential long leasehold property and commonhold property. On the website you can find a variety of useful reports on buying and living in leasehold and commonhold property, lease extensions, service charges and the right to manage.

31 Worship Street
London EC2A 2DX
Tel: 020 7374 5380
Fax: 020 7374 5373
Email: info@lease-advice.org.uk
Website: www.lease-advice.org.uk

CHARITIES

Electrical Safety Council (ESC)

The ESC is an independent charity committed to reducing deaths and injuries through electrical accidents at home and at work. It is only able to provide general electrical safety guidance, so if you require advice on a specific case, you should contact Consumer Direct (see Appendix 3: Useful Websites).

18 Buckingham Gate
London SW1E 6LB
Tel: 0870 040 0561
Fax: 0870 040 0560
Email: enquiries@electricalsafetycouncil.org.uk
Website: www.electricalsafetycouncil.org.uk

Shelter

Shelter is a housing charity that campaigns to end problems with homelessness and bad housing. On its website you can access useful information, advice and statistics about repossessions and possession orders in the UK.

88 Old Street
London EC1V 9HU
Tel: 0845 458 4590
Fax: 020 7505 2030
Email: info@shelter.org.uk
Website: www.shelter.org.uk

CREDIT REFERENCE AGENCIES

There are three main credit reference agencies in the UK. Contact them direct for more information.

Callcredit Plc

PO Box 491
Leeds LS3 1WZ
Tel: 0870 060 1414
Website: www.callcredit.co.uk

Equifax Plc

Credit File Advice Centre
PO Box 1140
Bradford BD1 5US

Tel: 0870 010 0583
Website: www.equifax.co.uk

Experian Limited

Consumer Help Service
PO Box 8000
Nottingham NG80 7WF
Tel: 0870 241 6212
Website: www.experian.co.uk

GOVERNMENT

Companies House

The main functions of Companies House are to incorporate and dissolve limited companies, examine and store company information, and make this information available to the public. You can find out more information about your commonhold association from Companies House.

Crown Way
Maindy
Cardiff CF14 3UZ
Tel: 0870 333 3636
Email: enquiries@companies-house.gov.uk
Website: www.companieshouse.gov.uk

Financial Ombudsman Service (FOS)

The FOS has been set up by Parliament to help to settle disputes between businesses providing financial services and their customers. Information about complaints and resolutions over mortgage arrears and possession orders can be obtained from this organisation.

South Quay Plaza
183 Marsh Wall
London E14 9SR
Tel: 020 7964 1000
Fax: 020 7964 1001
Email: complaint.info@financial-ombudsman.org.uk
Website: www.financial-ombudsman.org.uk

Financial Services Authority (FSA)

The FSA is the UK's financial watchdog that has been set up by the government to regulate financial services and protect consumer rights. Information about mortgages and what people should do if they cannot pay them is provided on its website, via its helpline or in booklets which can be downloaded or ordered online.

25 The North Colonnade
Canary Wharf
London E13 5HS
Consumer helpline: 0845 606 1234
Mortgage publications: 0845 456 1555
Email: consumerhelp@fsa.gov.uk
Website: www.moneymadeclear.fsa.gov.uk

Information Commissioner's Office (ICO)

The ICO will be able to offer advice and intervene if you have a problem with a credit reference agency.

Wycliffe House
Water Lane
Wilmslow
Cheshire SK9 5AF
Tel: 01625 545 745
Fax: 01625 524 510
Email: mail@ico.gsi.gov.uk
Website: www.informationcommissioner.gov.uk

Scottish Building Standards Agency (SBSA)

The SBSA was set up on 21 June 2004 as an executive agency of the Scottish Government. Its role is to prepare the building regulations and write guidance on how to meet the regulations. On the website you can find more information about the regulations and access the Certification Register, which is the only source of information on approved certifiers and approved bodies in Scotland.

Denholm House
Almondvale Business Park
Livingston EH54 6GA

Tel: 01506 600 400
Fax: 01506 600 401
Email: info@sbsa.gsi.gov.uk
Website: www.sbsa.gov.uk

PROFESSIONAL ASSOCIATIONS/TRADE BODIES

Council of Mortgage Lenders (CML)

The CML is the trade association for the mortgage lending industry in the UK. The organisation provides a range of general information for the consumer, including guides about home buying and selling, buy-to-let products and mortgage information and statistics.

Bush House
North West Wing
Aldwych
London WC2B 4PJ
Tel: 0845 373 6771
Email: info@cml.org.uk
Website: www.cml.org.uk

Council for Registered Gas Installers (CORGI)

CORGI is the national watchdog for gas safety in the UK. Its remit is to investigate gas safety-related complaints from the public and provide members of the public with details of local registered installers. On the website you can obtain useful information about gas safety in the home and find an inspector and installer in your area.

1 Elmwood
Chineham Park
Crockford Lane
Basingstoke
Hampshire RG24 8WG
Tel: 0800 915 0480
Fax: 0870 401 2600
Email: enquiries@trustcorgi.com
Website: www.trustcorgi.com

Electrical Contractors' Association (ECA)

The ECA represents electrical engineering and building services in the UK. You can search for a member in your area by using the online directory.

ESCA House
34 Palace Court
London W2 4HY
Tel: 020 7313 4800
Fax: 020 7221 7344
Email: info@eca.co.uk
Website: www.eca.co.uk

Heating Equipment Testing and Approval Scheme (HETAS)

HETAS is the official body recognised by the government to approve solid fuel heating appliances, fuels and services. You can find a registered installer by using the online database.

Orchard Business Centre
Stoke Orchard
Gloucestershire GL52 7RZ
Tel: 0845 634 5626
Email: info@hetas.co.uk
Website: www.hetas.co.uk

National Association of Estate Agents (NAEA)

The NAEA is the largest professional body for estate agents in the UK. It has over 10,000 members who are bound by a professional code of practice and rules of conduct. A list of members is available on its website.

Arbon House
6 Tournament Court
Edgehill Drive
Warwick CV34 6LG
Tel: 01926 496 800
Fax: 01926 417 788
Email: info@naea.co.uk
Website: www.naea.co.uk

National Inspection Council for Electrical Installation Contracting (NICEIC)

The NICEIC is an independent, non-profit making, voluntary regulatory body covering the UK. Useful information about electrical safety for the householder can be obtained from this organisation. You can access a list of approved contractors through its website.

Warwick House
Houghton Hall Park
Houghton Regis
Dunstable
Bedfordshire LU5 5ZX
Tel: 0870 013 0382
Fax: 01582 539 090
Email: enquiries@niceic.org.uk
Website: www.niceic.org.uk

Oil Firing Technical Association (OFTEC)

OFTEC promotes excellence in oil-fired heating and cooking. Householders can obtain useful information on using oil in the home and find an inspector and installer by using the online directory.

Foxwood House
Dobbs Lane
Kesgrave
Ipswich IP5 2QQ
Tel: 0845 65 85 080
Fax: 0845 65 85 181
Email: enquiries@oftec.org
Website: www.oftec.co.uk

Ombudsman for Estate Agents (OEA)

The OEA has been established to provide an independent and impartial facility for the resolution of complaints between members of the public and people who act as agents for buying and selling residential property. You can find contact details of members in your area from its website.

Beckett House
4 Bridge Street

Salisbury
Wiltshire SP1 2LX
Tel: 01722 333 306
Fax: 01722 332 296
Email: admin@oea.co.uk
Website: www.oea.co.uk

APPENDIX 3:
USEFUL WEBSITES

BANKING/FINANCE

HBOS Plc

www.hbosplc.com

On this website you can access information about the Halifax House Price Index, use the regional house price map and access the postcode calculator that enables you to find out about average house prices in your area. There is other useful housing research and historical housing data that you may find useful when you are conducting your market research.

Nationwide

www.nationwide.co.uk

On this website you can access the Nationwide House Price Calculator and useful reports and housing bulletins. It is possible to find out how the value of a property has changed over the years by entering the postcode into the calculator available on the website.

GOVERNMENT

Consumer Direct

www.consumerdirect.gov.uk

A government website that provides clear and practical advice on all kinds of consumer issues. This includes problems you may have with faulty household appliances, builders and contractors, or extended warranties. If you have a specific problem with a repossessed property, contact Consumer Direct by email or telephone to find out if it can help (tel. 0845 404 0506).

Land Registry

www.landregistry.gov.uk

On this site you can find out about average house prices throughout England and Wales, narrowing your search to specific postcode areas. If you are interested in finding out more about a specific property, there is a small fee for the service.

Registers of Scotland Executive Agency

www.ros.gov.uk

On this website you can obtain information about house prices in Scotland. There is a small fee for obtaining details about specific properties.

INDEPENDENT WATCHDOGS/OMBUDSMEN

British and Irish Ombudsman Association (BIOA)

www.bioa.org.uk

On this site you can find a list of ombudsmen and other complaint-handling bodies that may be able to help you if you have a complaint. You can search the online database by keyword, jurisdiction and category.

Energy Ombudsman

www.energy-ombudsman.org.uk

The ombudsman offers a free and independent service, investigating complaints in cases where customers and suppliers cannot agree. If you decide to use this service, you must have complained to the utility company first. A complaints form is available on its website.

Energywatch

www.energywatch.org.uk

Energywatch is an independent gas and electricity watchdog. It offers free and impartial advice for energy consumers and it will take up your case if you feel that you have been unfairly treated by your gas or electricity supplier. This tends to have more impact than when individuals try to fight the case themselves, and disputes can be resolved quickly when Energywatch are called in. More information is available on its website, or you can call the helpline for advice (tel. 0845 906 0708).

PROFESSIONAL ASSOCIATIONS/TRADE BODIES

National Association of Professional Inspectors and Testers (NAPIT)

www.napit.org.uk

All NAPIT members carrying out domestic work in the UK are part of the government's Trustmark scheme, which signifies that a business has insurance, good health and safety practices, and good customer care. Also, all NAPIT members are backed by a full six-year guarantee for the workmanship. You can find a member by using the online database.

Royal Institution of Chartered Surveyors (RICS)

www.rics.org

Here you can find a number of useful reports, bulletins and statistics on repossessions and housing market forecasts in the UK.

www.ricsfirms.com

This is the online database of RICS. You can use the quick search facility to obtain contact information of a chartered surveyor in your area, by entering the country, location and type of firm. Firms that are regulated by RICS have to follow strict rules of conduct, must ensure that members are fully trained, must have adequate professional indemnity insurance and must have a complaints handling procedure in place.

PROPERTY

FindaProperty.com

www.findaproperty.com

You can search for properties throughout the UK on this website and access property news, articles and 'how to' guides. Advice is offered on buying bargain properties, which may, from time to time, include repossessions.

Home.co.uk

www.home.co.uk

On this website you can access information about house prices in all parts of the UK since April 2000. You can also use the postcode calculator to find out house prices within your postcode. The service is free and provides a wide range of useful housing information for buyers, sellers and investors.

Primelocation.com

www.primelocation.com

This website enables you to register your property search details for property in the UK and abroad, for free. The website contains useful information about moving home, insurance, legal issues, property investment, and many other aspects of buying and selling houses. From time to time, it has information about buying repossessed property.

Propertyfinder.com

www.propertyfinder.com

This website enables you to register your details for free and it will send you email alerts of properties matching your description. Although it will not say whether properties are repossessed, you can find out whether this is the case by following the advice in this book. The website provides other useful advice about buying, selling and renovating your home.

GLOSSARY OF TERMS

Adverse credit

This is a term that is used in official financial documents to describe bad credit, i.e. someone who is considered to be a high risk to lenders because he has experienced financial difficulties in the past, has missed payments or had debt recovery proceedings started against him.

Arrears

This is used to describe when a borrower has missed one or more payments on his mortgage or loan, but has not yet defaulted on his loan.

Bid

This is the amount that someone bids for a property (the bidder). At auctions the auctioneer usually controls the amount by which the bids increase, although it is possible for the bidder to specify a different amount, if he so wishes. A 'sealed bid' process can be used to buy repossessed property. This is where all the offers are put in writing and, in theory, should all be opened at the same time. Other estate agents will ask for 'bids' on a repossessed property that can be made at any time up until the exchange of contracts.

Building regulations

These are a set of rules that have been approved by Parliament. They manage minimum standards of design and building work required for the construction of domestic, commercial and industrial buildings. They include regulations concerning the health and safety of people in or around the building, energy conservation, disabled access and facilities, fire safety, structure, drainage and ventilation.

By order of mortgagees

This term is used to describe the sale of a repossessed property and it tends to be used in auction catalogues and during the sale.

Capped mortgage

With this type of deal, repayments are variable and linked to the base rate, but they are 'capped' and will not go above a set level during the period of the deal.

Collared mortgage

This type of deal may be used in conjunction with a capped rate and/or tracker mortgage. Payments are variable, but will never fall below a set level.

Completion

This is the last stage of the purchasing process and is the date by which all funds are paid and all documentation is finalised. The house becomes the property of the purchaser on this date.

Consumer Credit Act

This is the law that governs personal loans and other types of credit agreements, such as hire purchase and credit cards. According to the Department for Business, Enterprise and Regulatory Reform (BERR), 'the 2006 Act establishes a fairer, clearer and more competitive market for consumer credit, updating consumer credit legislation that has been in place since the 1970s and making it more relevant to today's consumers'.

County Court Judgment (CCJ)

This is an order issued by a court to a person who has not satisfied payment to his creditors. The order is for an amount agreed between the debtor and creditor, or for an amount stipulated by the court. Unless the full amount of the judgment is paid within one month, the CCJ will be recorded on the Register of County Court Judgments for six years. This information is then used by lenders to decide whether someone should be given a loan or other credit. Incorrect information can be removed from the Register and once a debt has been paid, the entry can be marked 'satisfied'. The Scottish equivalent of a CCJ is a 'decree'.

Credit reference agency

There are three credit reference agencies that collect and collate information about the borrowing habits of adults in the UK. The information is used by lenders to check people's identity, their credit history and ongoing credit commitment, so that they can decide whether or not to lend them money or offer credit. Information is obtained from various sources, such as local authorities, banks, building societies and other lenders. By law, credit reference agencies must provide you with your statutory credit file, when asked, although they will request a payment for doing so.

Discounted mortgage

With this type of deal, payments are variable, but are set at a rate less than the standard rate for a set period of time.

Exchange of contracts

This is when the transfer of title/ownership of a property happens. At this time, the buyer signs the contract for sale and sends it to the seller, who also signs the document. Both parties are legally bound to complete the transfer, once the exchange has taken place, and they cannot pull out of the deal. The contract will list the fixtures that are to be included in the sale and it will specify a date for completion. Buyers should ensure that buildings insurance is arranged from this date.

Fixed mortgage

This is where repayments are set at a certain level for a fixed period of time, and they will usually revert back to the standard rate after the agreed period.

Impaired credit

This occurs when a borrower has experienced credit problems and is disqualified from using the products of mainstream lenders. An impaired credit mortgage is a specialist loan available for people with a history of credit problems. These can also be known as 'adverse credit loans'.

Individual Voluntary Agreement (IVA)

An IVA enables a person who is in debt to come to an agreement with his creditors by paying off a percentage of the debt over a specific period of time, thus avoiding bankruptcy or repossession. A regular payment plan is drawn up by a specialist practitioner who decides how much an individual can realistically afford to pay each month. Recently, there has been a great deal of media coverage about IVAs, in particular about companies exaggerating the amount of debt that can be wiped out.

Loan to Value (LTV)

This is the amount that a person wishes to borrow as a percentage of the purchase price or valuation (whichever is lower) and it is affected by the size of the deposit. Borrowers are likely to obtain a better deal if they have a lower LTV rate.

LPA receiver

An LPA receiver is a person appointed under the Law of Property Act 1925 to take charge of a mortgaged property by a lender whose loan is in default. This usually involves selling the property or collecting a rental income for the lender. An LPA receiver tends to be used in more complex situations, such as where a property developer is in arrears and has money secured on several properties.

Monetary Policy Committee (MPC)

The MPC is a Bank of England committee that meets each month to decide on the official interest rate in the UK. The Committee is made up of nine members – five internal and four external, with each member having expertise in the field of economics and monetary policy. A representative from the Treasury also sits with the Committee at its meetings.

Money judgment

This is a decision made by a judge that enables creditors to recover the total sum due, including arrears and all other costs. A money judgment can be attached to a possession order, which means that someone loses his home and has to pay arrears.

Mortgage Indemnity Guarantee (MIG)

This is insurance that provides the lender with protection against a borrower defaulting on a loan, covering the lender for the extra amount lent that may not be recovered if the property is repossessed and sold. This can happen in cases where the value of the property has fallen since the loan was taken out. This type of payment tends to be required if the LTV is higher than a certain figure, usually over 90 per cent, although this varies between lenders. The MIG premium can be a one-off payment paid by the borrower when the loan is taken out, or it can be added to the mortgage advance, which means that interest will be charged on the MIG. The amount of premium is based on the value of the property and the LTV ratio. Some lenders refer to this payment as a 'Higher Loan to Value fee' or a 'higher lending charge'.

Mortgage payment protection insurance

This is a comprehensive insurance policy that will cover your mortgage repayments over a specified length of time, if you are unable to meet the payments yourself. This could be due to accident, disability, illness or unemployment.

Order for sale

This is a decision made by a judge that enables a homeowner to try to sell his property privately, within a certain timescale, before it is repossessed by the lender.

Possession order

This is a decision made by a judge that enables the lender to repossess its property. The court will give a date by which time the property must become vacant, which is usually 28 days; although, in certain circumstances, it could be up to six weeks.

Self-certification mortgage

This is a process through which borrowers, usually those who are self-employed or those who are unable to provide evidence of their income, are able to state their level of income without providing documentary evidence. In certain circumstances, an accountant may be required to back up statements. This type of mortgage will almost certainly require a larger deposit than other types of mortgage.

Standard variable rate mortgage

This is where payments go up and down when the lender's mortgage rate changes, usually in line with the Bank of England base rate. Standard variable rate with cashback is also offered, which means that once you have taken out the loan, you will receive a sum of cash, which could amount to five per cent of your loan.

Suspended possession order

This is a decision by a judge that enables a possession order to be suspended if a borrower agrees to certain conditions, such as making payments towards his arrears. If these conditions are breached, the lender can apply to the court immediately for possession.

Tracker mortgage

This is a variable rate loan which tracks changes in the base rate, at an agreed rate for an agreed amount of time.

Voluntary possession declaration

This is a document that a borrower is asked to sign to confirm that he has agreed to surrender his property and that he understands that he is still liable for all of the mortgage payments and costs until the property is sold.

Index